For the Love of God

For the Love of God
NGOs and Religious Identity in a Violent World

Shawn Teresa Flanigan

Kumarian Press
An Imprint of Stylus Publishing

*For Mounah, who taught me we are all much more
alike than we could ever imagine, and
for Boyd, who loves books.*

For the Love of God:
NGOs and Religious Identity in a Violent World

Published 2010 in the United States of America by Kumarian Press
22883 Quicksilver Drive, Sterling, VA 20166 USA

Copyedit by Connie Day
Proofread by Sue Boshers, WordMagic
Index by Robert Swanson
Design and production by Rosanne Schloss, Pro Production
The text of this book is set in 11/14.5 Times Roman

∞ The paper used in this publication meets the minimum requirements of the American National Standard for Information Sciences—Permanence of Paper for Printed Library Materials, ANSI Z39.48-1984.

Library of Congress Cataloging-in-Publication Data

Flanigan, Shawn.
For the love of God : NGOs and religious identity in a violent world / by
    Shawn Flanigan.
        p. cm.
    Includes bibliographical references and index.
    ISBN 978-1-56549-307-0 (pbk. : alk. paper) — ISBN 978-1-56549-308-7
        (cloth : alk. paper)
    1. Faith-based human services—Developing countries—Evaluation.
2. Non-governmental organizations—Developing countries—Evaluation.
3. Community development—Religious aspects—Evaluation. I. Title.
    HV530.F548 2010
    361.7'5091724—dc22
                                                                    2009022069

Contents

Acknowledgments

First and foremost, I would like to thank the NGO staff members in Bosnia and Herzegovina, Lebanon, and Sri Lanka who were kind enough to take time out of their busy schedules to speak with me and allow me to observe their important work. Many of my interview participants welcomed me into their lives with food, drink, and open arms, and this project would have been impossible without their candor and patience.

This book grew out of my doctoral dissertation, and I owe a debt of gratitude to Victor Asal, Judith R. Saidel, and Frank Thompson for their critical feedback and constant support of my work. My field work in Bosnia and Herzegovina was funded by the Individual Advanced Research Opportunity (IARO) program of the International Research and Exchanges Board (IREX), and I am grateful for this support. My field work in Lebanon and Sri Lanka was supported in part by the START Center at the University of Maryland, and I would like to thank Gary LaFree, Kathie Smarick, and Kate Worboys for the START Center's financial support and professional mentoring. The first seeds for this research project were planted when I was a Fulbright researcher in Romania in 2002–2003, and I am grateful to the United States Fulbright Program and the Romanian-American Fulbright Commission for their funding. I would like to thank the Abbass and Abdel Samad families for their hospitality in Lebanon, and I thank Ramez Abbass, Mounah Abdel Samad, and Rodi Jammoul for their assistance with Arabic language interpretation. I thank Mirjiana Milanovic for her friendship, for her patience as my Bosnian language instructor, and for her assistance with Bosnian language interpretation.

My great appreciation goes to Jim Lance of Kumarian Press for his guidance and patience in mentoring a new and inexperienced author such as myself. I am grateful to Stuart Henry for his feedback on my book proposal and for his constant professional guidance, and to Shawn Gaskari for his careful editing of this volume.

No research project is possible without the enthusiasm, laughter, patience, and practical support of a wide array of family and friends. I offer my utmost gratitude to Lisa Alison, Norma Anderson, Carrie Barnett, Debbie Brown, Miranda Cully, James Dean, Tim Flanigan, Cecilia Gutierrez, Dawn Guinan, Deneen Hatmaker, Glen Johnson, Paul Kaplan, Tudor Kovacs, Dan Lynch, Najib Maalouf, Karl Rethemeyer, George Richardson, Micheal Stratton, Istvan Vanyolos, Roli Varma, all of my classmates and the faculty and staff at Rockefeller College at the University at Albany, and my colleagues at San Diego State University. Finally, I want to express my gratitude and love to all of my family, both in the United States and in the Middle East, and above all to Mounah.

1

NGOs, Religious Identity, and Violence in the Developing World

The faithful have provided assistance to the less fortunate in their communities for centuries. Yet in recent years, policymakers have given greater attention to faith-based organizations (FBOs) providing health and social services. Governments worldwide are beginning to recognize the social policy potential of harnessing the generosity of the faithful. In the United States, the recent increase in attention to FBOs has been attributed to President George W. Bush, whose first Executive Order was to create the Office of Faith-Based and Community Initiatives. However, in the United States conservative politicians hardly have a monopoly on support for provision of faith-based services. Just as George W. Bush continued to use Executive Orders to increase the scale of faith-based initiatives throughout his presidency, President Bill Clinton also was a staunch supporter of faith-based service provision, and President Barack Obama began discussing his desire to expand Bush's faith-based initiative early in his presidential campaign. In the United Kingdom, both Conservative Party and New Labour Party politicians have expressed an interest in increasing the role of FBOs in service delivery, in spite of an increased secularization of British society since World War II.

In 2002 President George W. Bush mandated that the United States Agency for International Development (USAID) expand religious non-profits' access to its grants and contracts, and the United Kingdom's

Department for International Development (DFID) has conducted substantial research on the role of religion and FBOs in development. In contrast to prior development discourse that emphasized the legal separation of church and state in liberal democracy-building efforts, major donor organizations such as the World Bank have begun to acknowledge the importance of religious organizations in the lives of the poor and to recognize the utility of partnering with FBOs in development. Regardless of political leaning, many policymakers around the world are singing the praises of FBOs as partners in domestic social policy and in international development.[1]

Those in favor of increasing support for faith-based service provision speak of the numerous benefits of religion in service environments. Supporters assert that FBO staff members are more caring, compassionate, and supportive because they are motivated by religious faith. FBOs are viewed as being more strongly rooted in local communities, and they are seen as having desirable moral and spiritual qualities that make them better equipped to work with certain difficult-to-serve populations. International FBOs working in developing countries sometimes are perceived as exhibiting greater long-term commitment to local communities than secular nongovernmental organizations (NGOs) exhibit. Indeed, research demonstrates a strong positive correlation between individuals' religious practice and improvements in their health and well-being, and there is a growing body of research demonstrating the effectiveness of faith-based health and social services.[2] Could FBOs be the panacea needed to cure the ills of development practice?

Without diminishing the benefits that FBOs have to offer the field of international development, this book advises caution to those who would hastily embrace the role of FBOs in development efforts. Instead, this book takes the critical perspective that FBOs must be incorporated into international development efforts with careful attention to the religious traditions, social context, and political history of the specific country and region where development work is being conducted. FBOs may offer advantages as service providers, but they are not a cure-all, and they can be particularly problematic in contexts of religious and ethnic conflict. Whereas much of the research on religious identity and nonprofit organizations has been focused on Europe and the United States, I argue that religious identity plays a much different role in the context of developing countries experiencing religious conflict.

Specifically, central to this book is the argument that in contexts of ethnic and religious violence, *FBOs may mirror, reinforce, and reproduce societal divisions* that are present in the cultures in which they operate. This is because the mechanisms that promote and channel collective violence not only affect society at large, but also influence the behavior of FBO staff members and the behavior of the poor in communities that have experienced violent religious conflict. As this book will discuss in greater detail, the politics of collective violence influence the behavior of FBO staff and low-income community members in ways that have important implications for inclusion and exclusion in health and social services. The risk of exclusion and coercion in poor communities is exacerbated by the power dynamics that are inherent in providing and receiving aid. When service recipients experience exclusion or coercion during their efforts to meet their basic human needs, these experiences can have a significant impact on political learning, thus influencing how the poor perceive NGOs, civil society, and the state. This book explores that dynamic by examining FBOs in Bosnia and Herzegovina, Lebanon, and Sri Lanka.

Religion as Motivation for Charity and Violence

As early as Weber and Durkheim, sociologists studying religion have recognized the role that religious belief plays in motivating human behavior and giving rise to communal activity. Sociology of religion has been incorporated into theorizing on a number of subjects often associated with the nonprofit sector, including altruism, civic engagement, and civil society. Religious identity and beliefs are often a motivation for charity and altruism, and research has shown that faith plays an important role in motivating the employees and volunteers of faith-based nonprofit service providers. As J. Bruce Nichols notes in his examination of nonprofits providing international humanitarian relief, "it was religious motivation that inspired relief workers to travel halfway around the world and serve their fellow human beings" (1988, p. 234).

Although a great deal of academic research focuses on religion as a motivation for volunteering and service provision by Christian organizations, it is important to emphasize that the teachings of many religious traditions provide motivation for charity and service. Generosity and service to others have central importance in Buddhism. Hinduism makes giving a duty, though charity is often highly structured by social context such as caste. Sikhism emphasizes that joyful service to others, along with devotional praise and ethical living, is essential to accomplishing one's goal of becoming more God-centered. Similarly, in Islam charity, hospitality, and philanthropy are seen as ways of achieving nearness to God. Philanthropy is central to Judaism as well, and many writers on the subject assert that Judaism was the first religion to make charity, or tzedakah, a religious obligation. Aside from the lofty teachings of many of the world's religious traditions, a number of studies have shown that individual religious congregations often find faith, mission, and action in the community to be inextricably linked.[3]

However, just as religious motivation for charity and service provision is common to many religions, all major religious traditions have at times used religion as a rationale for violence. Religion often provides a motivation, justification, organization, and worldview that allow for public acts of violence, with religious violence often framed on a global scale in terms of a cosmic war between good and evil. Religious conflicts burgeoned between 1950 and 1996, increasing from 33 to 47 percent of all conflicts worldwide. Not only is religion an identifiable motivation for violence around the world, but in many contexts religion is so profoundly intertwined with economic, ideological, territorial, and ethnic motivations for violence that each aspect becomes difficult to isolate. Of course, religious identity in and of itself does not motivate violent behavior. Exclusion and grievance often serve as a catalyst, and much political violence originates from the fact that groups are excluded from political and social participation in mainstream society.[4]

The Politics of Collective Violence and FBO Service Provision

Given this, one should not be surprised to find that FBOs operating in contexts of religious violence are influenced not only by their faith's teachings of generosity and service, but also by the religious community's experiences of violence and exclusion. Based on theories regarding the politics of collective violence, I argue that the behavior of FBOs and potential service recipients is different when these organizations provide services in societies that have experienced religious violence. In contexts of religious conflict there is an increase in polarization and boundary activation. The term *polarization* refers to a widening of social or political space between claimants in a contentious episode. Polarization promotes collective violence by making us-them boundaries more salient. As these boundaries between in-groups and out-groups become more salient, social interactions increasingly organize around these boundaries, and actors increasingly differentiate between within-boundary and across-boundary interactions. This process is called boundary activation. The relationship among polarization, boundary activation, and collective violence is dynamic and has the capacity to reproduce itself in a vicious circle. Polarization and boundary activation can lead to collective violence, and afterward those experiences of violence and exclusion lead to further polarization and even more highly activated boundaries among groups.[5]

Boundary activation influences the behavior of FBOs and the poor in communities that have experienced violent religious conflict, and it results in less inclusive service provision. FBOs are less inclusive of community members of other faiths as a consequence of boundary activation's influence on the FBO itself and/or boundary activation's influence on potential service recipients. Because of an increased awareness of across-boundary interactions, FBOs may overtly discriminate against members of other religions or ethnicities, or they may conduct less outreach to members of other ethno-religious groups. In addition, because boundary activation causes social interactions to increasingly organize around group identity, potential service recipients of other ethnicities and religions may be apprehensive about seeking services from the FBO, even if the FBO would be willing to provide them with services.

Polarization and boundary activation have a more powerful influence on the inclusiveness of local indigenous FBOs, but international FBOs are affected as well. The staff of international FBOs typically have not been involved in the local conflict and thus are relatively unaffected by local polarization and boundary activation. However, these mechanisms of collective violence are quite salient for the populations they seek to serve. Potential service recipients assess whether international FBOs are socially located inside or outside activated boundaries, and thus they determine whether or not it is advisable to seek assistance from the organization. The result is that the FBO sector may mirror, reinforce, and reproduce societal divisions that have been generated by ethnic and religious violence, whether intentionally or unintentionally.

Power and Coercion in Service Provision

The risk of exclusion from services in poor communities, and the risk of evangelical coercion, is exacerbated by the power dynamics that are inherent in providing and receiving aid. The prevailing assumption that service providers and service recipients always have aligned interests is simplistic and often false. Such assumptions ignore the intrinsic role of power in service relationships. Power plays a central role in relationships between FBO staff and service recipients, and although service recipients face a critical power disadvantage in many service contexts, this power disadvantage may be heightened in contexts of conflict.[6]

As Emerson notes in his theory of reciprocal power-dependence relations, "the power of A over B is equal to, and based upon, the dependence of B upon A" (1962, p. 33). Therefore, the amount of power a health or social service provider has over the service recipient is a function of the service recipient's ability to obtain aid elsewhere. In many cases, the service recipient's ability to obtain aid elsewhere is quite low. Even in Europe and the United States, many nonprofit agencies have a monopoly within their service area, a condition that is thought to be much more prevalent in developing countries. In fact, all of the NGO staff interviewed for this book indicated that their organization was the sole provider of certain services in some communities. Therefore, many poor community members in the developing world have little ability to seek assistance from multiple service providers, and thus they suffer a serious power disadvantage in comparison to an organization that is the sole provider of a needed service. When a service recipient is dependent on a particular agency or organization for aid, the recipient lacks power, liberty, and true choice.[7]

This power disadvantage has at least two important implications for this study, one related to exclusion and one related to coercion. Because of the prevalence of sole service provision, the poor are often in a position where they must choose between seeking services from a particular provider and going without services entirely. This is hardly a real choice when the services one speaks of include food aid, urgent medical care, clothing, shelter, and other goods and services essential to meeting basic human needs. However, in contexts of conflict, polarization and boundary activation make this decision more complex. If boundary activation causes an FBO to intentionally exclude members of other faiths, or if it causes community members to be apprehensive about seeking services from FBOs of other faiths, this can have dire implications for the ability of the poor to meet their basic needs. Specific segments of the population may be systematically excluded from services, either because of the discriminatory behavior of the FBO or because of their own choice to avoid the organization.

The power disadvantage for poor community members also has important implications for the coercive potential of FBOs. Supply-side theories of the nonprofit sector suggest that the emergence of nonprofit organizations has less to do with the demand for nonprofit services than with the supply of entrepreneurs who are committed to establish those services. These theorists suggest that one of the most likely sources of such supply is religious institutions, particularly in circumstances where religious competition exists. It is argued that religious orders create nonprofit institutions not entirely because of altruism, but for the instrumental purpose of winning new adherents. The formation of NGOs is thus a way in which religious groups can win devotees to their cause, and community members with desperate needs for education, health care, or other basic supports will come to accept the faith of those who sponsor such services. Empirical evidence of FBO efforts to evangelize has been found in Brazil, Egypt, Ghana, India, Romania, Thailand, the United Kingdom, and the United States, and in the research conducted for this book as well. From a client-focused perspective, this raises ethical issues when one considers the notable power that administrators of social programs hold over recipients. Staff of organizations that are sole service providers may use this power to encourage conversion among service recipients of other faiths, or community members may choose to avoid evangelic organizations, thus denying themselves much-needed services. Particularly in contexts of conflict where religious polarization and boundary activation are high, attempts at conversion may be seen as especially threatening.[8]

Of course, the mere presence of a power advantage does not necessarily mean that the more powerful party will use its power at the expense of the less powerful party. The use of power is governed by values and norms. FBO staff members are constrained by their organizations' rules and regulations, and many health and human services staff are socialized to the norms and ethics of their profession. However, there are particular risks that may be heightened in the developing world and in contexts of violence. Traditionally, nonprofit organizations' services have often been provided by those motivated by a moral or religious calling rather than by professionals. Although professionalism is becoming the norm in the nonprofit sector in Europe and the United States, the developing world may be more susceptible to philanthropic amateurism. This philanthropic amateurism can undermine the ability of professional norms and ethics to constrain the use of power. Many FBOs have rules and regulations that prohibit evangelism, but there is evidence that such rules are often ignored by front-line service providers who are motivated by their personal faith. Finally, rules and regulations that promote inclusive, noncoercive service provision simply may not be appropriate if an FBO has an organizational goal of evangelism, if it has a goal of serving members only of its own religious community, or when the use of organizational power is shaped by the politics of collective violence.[9]

Service Settings as Site of Political Learning

Why do recipients' experiences of the service system matter? Other than individual experiences of exclusion or barriers to access, why do the experiences of service recipients have implications for international development policy? I argue that recipients' experiences with service systems are important not only in the context of concerns about distributive justice, but because social welfare programs serve as sites for political learning. In his 2002 book *Unwanted Claims,* Joe Soss argues that service recipients learn lessons about government and political demand making through their experiences in service systems. Those lessons become part of service recipients' perception of government at large. Soss's research is paralleled by a large body of research on the important role that nonprofit organizations and voluntary associations play as vehicles for political participation. In the context of international development, foreign policy in Europe and the United States increasingly emphasizes democratization and targets countries where vast percentages of the population live in poverty. If service recipients are excluded by nonprofit service providers on the grounds of ethnic or religious identity, or if the service providers' efforts at evangelizing make them feel that their ethno-religious identity is not respected, this observation can extend to their perception of nonprofit organizations, civil society, and government as a whole. Particularly in the case of nascent states, poor citizens' negative experiences as service recipients and as participants in nonprofit organizations may cause them to view civil society and the state as enforcing and reproducing ethnic and religious divisions.[10]

However, recipients' feelings of efficacy and levels of political engagement vary across program designs. In his study of social service programs in the United States, Soss found that recipients who did not fear losing access to benefits perceived government as a whole as being more responsive and concerned with the needs of citizens. In addition, service recipients in systems that required client participation in decision-making processes had higher feelings of efficacy and higher levels of political engagement, even outside the service environment. This observation echoes assertions by many scholars and practitioners that nonprofit organizations serve as "incubators" of democratic citizenship competencies, allowing individuals to gain important organizational and communication skills that prepare them for political participation. Soss's study, combined with research on nonprofit organizations and political engagement, leads one to believe that the experiences of citizens receiving development aid can have an important impact on their perception of and engagement with their own civil society institutions and government. If European countries and the United States are truly concerned with supporting effective democracies in the developing world, they should take a strong interest in ensuring that recipients have fair and equitable experiences when receiving services. In addition, citizens' experiences receiving development aid certainly have an important impact on their perception of the United States and European donor governments. A 2005 survey of 3,000 respondents from Indonesia, Pakistan, and a number of Arab countries indicated that individuals who felt that the United States government had a foreign policy goal of spreading Christianity were significantly more supportive of attacks on the United States and of jihadist groups in general. Reducing exclusionary or evangelic practices by service providers should help to ensure that service recipients have fair and equitable experiences when receiving services and that they feel their cultural and religious beliefs are respected and honored.[11]

The Organization of the Book

This book examines the importance of religious identity in nonprofit health and social service provision in Lebanon, Sri Lanka, and Bosnia and Herzegovina based on fieldwork conducted in each country between 2005 and 2007. Bosnia and Herzegovina is an important case because of its recent history of ethno-religious politicide during the 1990s. Lebanon is a valuable case because of its history of religious conflict. The 1975–1990 Lebanese civil war between Christian and Muslim militants has left behind a legacy of tension in the country, and sectarian divisions still play an important role in national politics and government representation. Finally, Sri Lanka is used as a case because of its longer than 25-year civil war between the Sri Lankan government and the Tamil Tigers. Sri Lanka's war is an ethnic conflict between the Sinhalese majority and the Tamil minority, but these groups are also divided along religious lines and use religious symbolism in their political rhetoric and violent attacks.

Based on site visits to NGOs in each country and on interviews with more than one hundred management-level NGO staff members, this book examines the ways in which religious identity influences the work of faith-based nonprofit organizations and makes their health and social services unique in their community. The staff members who were interviewed worked for both local country-based NGOs and international European- and US-based NGOs. Although an examination of congregational service provision or service provision by informal groups undoubtedly would be interesting, this book focuses specifically on formal organizations that are legally registered as NGOs or the equivalent in their country of origin. Interviews were conducted with staff of both faith-based and secular NGOs. Because the term *faith-based* is interpreted differently by a variety of scholars and professionals, in this book organizations are referred to as faith-based if the organization's staff self-identified the NGO as faith-based during the interview process.[12]

It is important to note that this book squarely focuses on the role that religious identity plays within FBOs, as described by management-level FBO staff. Studies focusing on front-line staff within FBOs, on the communities in which FBOs are based, or on relationships between FBOs and local or national government entities undeniably would be of great interest and value. A study focused on service recipients would provide fascinating and useful information, particularly regarding the extent to which service recipients experience exclusion, coercion, or evangelism when receiving services. However, these topics are beyond the scope of this book. Studies using methods other than interviews with staff members would provide useful information but might lack the richness and depth that personal story-telling about the motivating aspects of faith provides.

The Western bias that colors this examination is inescapable. I am a white female from the United States, trained mostly by white males, in a discipline created by white males. Although I do not adhere to any religious faith, I have been raised in a culture where Judeo-Christian philosophies are dominant. I have a normative commitment to republican ideals of liberty, equality, and popular sovereignty. I hold the normative belief that all human beings have an unalienable right to meet their basic social and economic needs with their dignity intact. The responses that the interview participants provided were undoubtedly influenced by my class, education level, gender, and nationality, as well as their own. However, I have sent my work to my interview participants for review, and I have incorporated their corrections and suggestions humbly and gratefully. I have made an effort to acknowledge my social position and my biases in this project from the outset, and I have tried to remain mindful of these throughout the analysis. Based on the candid, sensitive, and often controversial information the interview participants were willing to share with me, I am hopeful that I have painted an accurate and useful portrait of FBOs working in Bosnia and Herzegovina, Lebanon, and Sri Lanka.

Finally, though this book often adopts a critical stance toward FBO service provision, I want to make it clear that I have the utmost respect and admiration for the FBO professionals I met during the course of my field research. FBO assistance undoubtedly has improved the lives of service recipients in numerous ways. This book should not be understood as a condemnation of FBOs or as a call to end government support of FBO service provision. Instead, I advocate careful attention to local religious traditions, social context, and political history when incorporating FBOs into international development efforts. Adopting a careful approach to FBO funding and professional practice can amplify the benefits of FBO service provision and help minimize the potential pitfalls.

The pages that follow present information I gathered in each of the countries where I conducted my fieldwork. Chapter 2 discusses FBOs in Lebanon, Chapter 3 discusses Sri Lanka, and Chapter 4 discusses Bosnia and Herzegovina. Chapter 5 takes a broader look at the role that mechanisms of collective violence play in FBO service provision in all three countries. Then it concludes with practical recommendations for development professionals, NGO staff, and public and private donors and contractors.

Notes

1. For more on government support for FBOs in the United Kingdom, see Margaret Harris, Peter Halfpenny, and Colin Rochester, "A Social Policy Role for Faith-Based Organisations? Lessons from the UK Jewish Voluntary Sector," *Journal of Social Policy* 32, no. 1 (2003): 93–112. For more on DFID's and the World Bank's stance on FBOs, see Gerard Clarke, "Agents of Transformation? Donors, Faith-Based Organsations and International Development," *Third World Quarterly* 28, no. 1 (2007): 77–96.

2. For more on the distinctive characteristics of faith-based service providers, see Tamsin Bradley, "Does Compassion Bring Results? A Critical Perspective on Faith and Development," *Culture and Religion* 6, no. 3 (2005): 337–51; Mark Chaves and William Tsitsos, "Congregations and Social Services: What They Do, How They Do It, and with Whom," *Nonprofit & Voluntary Sector Quarterly* 30, no. 4 (2001): 660–83; and Helen Rose Ebaugh, Paula F. Pipes, Janet Saltzman Chafetz, and Martha Daniels, "Where's the Religion? Distinguishing Faith-Based from Secular Social Service Agencies," *Journal for the Scientific Study of Religion* 42, no. 3 (2003): 411–26. For more on the effectiveness of FBOs, see Robert Fischer, "In God We Trust, All Others Bring Data: Assessing the State of Outcomes Measurement for Faith-Based and Community-Based Programming," in *Innovations in Effective Compassion: Compendium of Research Papers Presented at the Faith-Based and Community Initiatives Conference on Research, Outcomes, and Evaluation* (Washington, DC: US Department of Health and Human Services, 2008), 179–211. For more on the relationship among religiosity, positive behaviors, and health outcomes, see Byron R. Johnson, Ralph Brett Tompkins, and Derek Webb, *Objective Hope—Assessing the Effectiveness of Faith-Based Organizations: A Review of the Literature* (Philadelphia: University of Pennsylvania, Center for Research on Religion and Urban Civil Society, 2002). For an assessment of the current state of evidence-based research on the effectiveness of faith-based service provision, see Fischer, 2008. For more on professionalism, philanthropic amateurism, and the social construction of FBO service recipients, see Lester Salamon, *Partners in Public Service: Government-Nonprofit Relations in the Modern Welfare State* (Baltimore, MD: Johns Hopkins University Press, 1995); and Bradley, 2005.

3. For early treatises on the sociology of religion, see Émile Durkheim, *The Elementary Forms of the Religious Life* (New York: The Free Press, 1954); and Max Weber, *The Sociology of Religion* (Boston, MA: Beacon Press, 1963). For more on religious motivation in humanitarian aid, see John Bruce Nichols, *The Uneasy Alliance: Religion, Refugee*

Work, and U.S. Foreign Policy (New York: Oxford University Press, 1988). For more on religious teachings about charity and service, see Warren F. Ilchman, Stanley Katz, and Edward L. Queen II, *Philanthropy in the World's Traditions* (Bloomington: Indiana University Press, 1998).

4. For more on religion as a rationale for violence, see Mark Juergensmeyer, *Terror in the Mind of God: The Global Rise of Religious Violence* (Berkeley: University of California Press, 2003); and Gregory F. Treverton, Heather S. Gregg, Daniel Gibran, and Charles W. Yost, *Exploring Religious Conflict* (Santa Monica, CA: RAND Corporation, 2005). For estimates on increases in religious conflict, see Jonathan Fox, "Religion and State Failure: An Examination of the Extent and Magnitude of Religious Conflict from 1950 to 1996," *International Political Science Review* 25, no. 1 (2004): 55–64. For more on exclusion as a source of grievance and violence, see Ted Gurr, *People Versus States: Minorities at Risk in the New Century* (Washington, DC: United States Institute of Peace Press, 2000).

5. For more on the politics of collective violence, see Charles Tilly, *The Politics of Collective Violence* (New York: Cambridge University Press, 2003).

6. For more on the role of power in service settings, see Yeheskel Hasenfeld, *Human Service Organizations* (Englewood Cliffs, NJ: Prentice-Hall, 1983); and Yeheskel Hasenfeld, "Power in Social Work Practice," *Social Service Review* 61, no. 3 (1987): 469–83.

7. For more on power-dependence theory, see Richard M. Emerson, "Power-Dependence Relations," *American Sociological Review* 27 (1962): 31–41. For more on the role of power in service settings, see Hasenfeld, 1987.

8. For more on recruiting religious adherents as a motivation for service provision, see Nancy T. Ammerman, *Doing Good in American Communities: Congregations and Service Organizations Working Together* (Hartford, CT: Hartford Institute for Religious Research, 2001); Helmut Anheier and Lester Salamon, *The Nonprofit Sector in the Developing World* (Manchester, England: Manchester University Press,

1998); John P. Bartkowski, *The Promise and Peril of Charitable Choice: Faith-Based Initiatives in Mississippi* (Cambridge, MA: Harvard University Press, 2001); Shawn Teresa Flanigan, "Paying for God's Work: A Rights-Based Examination of Faith-Based NGOs in Romania," *VOLUNTAS: International Journal of Voluntary and Nonprofit Organizations* 18, no. 2 (2007): 156–75; Estelle James, *The Nonprofit Sector in International Perspective: Studies in Comparative Culture and Policy* (New York: Oxford University Press, 1989); Stephen V. Monsma and Carolyn M. Mounts, *Working Faith: How Religious Organizations Provide Welfare-to-Work Services* (Philadelphia, PA: Center for Religion and Urban Civil Society, 2002); and Susan Rose-Ackerman, "Altruism, Nonprofits and Economic Theory," *Journal of Economic Literature* 34, no. 2 (1996): 701–26.

9. For more on power in service settings, see Hasenfeld, 1987. For more on philanthropic amateurism, see Salamon, 1995. For more on differences between the behavior of FBO managers and that of FBO front-line staff, see Flanigan, 2007.

10. For more on service settings as sites of political learning, see Joe Soss, *Unwanted Claims: The Politics of Participation in the U.S. Welfare System* (Ann Arbor: University of Michigan Press, 2002). For more on nonprofits and political participation, see Judith R. Saidel, "Nonprofit Organizations, Political Engagement, and Public Policy," in *Exploring Organizations and Advocacy,* ed. Elizabeth J. Reid and Maria D. Montilla (Washington, DC: Urban Institute, 2002), 1–18.

11. Saidel, 2002; Soss, 2002; Stephen Weber, *Perceptions of the United States and Support for Violence Against America* (College Park, MD: National Consortium for the Study of Terrorism and Responses to Terrorism, 2006).

12. For more on the lack of consensus in the academic community regarding classification of FBOs, see Carol J. De Vita and Sarah Wilson, *Faith-Based Initiatives: Sacred Deeds and Secular Dollars* (Washington, DC: The Urban Institute, the Hauser Center for Nonprofit Organizations, 2001); Ebaugh, Pipes, Saltzman Chafetz, and Daniels, 2003;

Thomas Jeavons, "Identifying Characteristics of 'Religious' Organizations: An Exploratory Proposal," in *Sacred Companies: Organizational Aspects of Religion and Religious Aspects of Organizations,* ed. N. J. Demerath III, Peter Dobkin Hall, Terry Schmitt, and Rhys H. Williams (New York: Oxford University Press, 1998); and Steven Rathgeb Smith and Michael R. Sosin, "The Varieties of Faith-Related Agencies," *Public Administrative Review* 61 (2001): 651–69.

2

Sectarian Social Welfare

Faith and Faction
in Lebanon's NGO Sector

Situated between Syria and Israel on the Mediterranean Sea, Lebanon is a country where, as the Lebanese proudly proclaim, on the same day you can spend your morning skiing in the mountains and your afternoon lounging at a seaside resort. Although Lebanon is a small country—it is less than 75 percent of the size of the US state of Connecticut—it has been the site of numerous conflicts in the Middle East, often dominating the headlines of the evening news. The country is home to seventeen legally recognized religious sects, who unfortunately have not lived together peacefully. As a result, one could debate whether Lebanon is more famous for the 1975–1990 civil war between religious militia groups or for the activities of the Shiite militant group Hezbollah, a political organization that is categorized by the United States government as a terrorist organization. Both of these claims to fame, as well as clashes over Syrian intervention in internal politics and attacks by alleged al Qaeda operatives in the country, have visited political strife, violence, and economic difficulty on the Lebanese people. However, in addition to being a source of conflict, Lebanon's religious heterogeneity is given credit by some for generating one of the strongest and best-developed voluntary sectors in the Arab world.[1] Lebanon has a vibrant civil society sector, which includes secular nonprofit service providers and many faith-based service providers from the country's diverse religious sects.

Violence in Lebanon and the Salience of Sect

Prior to 1975, Lebanon had been characterized by years of violent but limited conflicts between Palestinians, Lebanese security forces, rival Muslim and Christian gangs in Beirut, and Maronite Christian militias. The Maronites, a denomination of Roman Catholics of the Eastern Rite who live predominantly in the Middle East, are the largest Christian sect in Lebanon. An April 1975 assassination attempt on Maronite leader Pierre Gemayel and subsequent retribution killings escalated beyond control, marking the beginning of Lebanon's civil war. Lebanon's civil war undoubtedly was shaped by dimensions of nation and class, for there were conflicts between militarized Palestinians and Maronite Christians, as well as between "poor Muslims" seeking to address uneven socio-economic development and "rich Christians" interested in preserving the status quo. However, Lebanon's protracted conflict quickly took on religious overtones. Hostages were taken based on the religious sect marked on their identity cards, and many were subsequently raped, tortured, mutilated, and killed. Injuries, defacement, destruction, and other atrocities of war were colored by religious symbolism. Women were targeted on the basis of the sexual stereotypes other sects had about their religious group, churches and mosques were burned, and cemeteries were bulldozed. As the war continued, large-scale sect-based massacres became more common, and in urban areas some neighborhoods were destroyed entirely, leaving residents with nowhere to return.[2]

An important aspect of the civil war is that few religious communities in Lebanon remained untouched by violence. There was fierce fighting between Maronites and Muslims, Maronites and Druze, and Muslims and Druze, and conflicts even occurred between Sunni and Shiite Muslims. Maronites, Druze, Sunnis, and Shiites played the most central role in the conflict, but the Orthodox and Catholic communities played an active if marginal role as well. The theories of collective violence discussed in Chapter 1 suggest that this history of collective violence among religious groups makes religious identity more salient, leads to the activation of religious boundaries, and causes social interactions increasingly to organize around religious sect. Religious identity has been a major reference point for social interaction within the Lebanese population since the time of Ottoman rule. Religious identity plays a strong role in social life in Lebanon, with each sect having the legal right to determine its own procedures for acknowledging and dissolving marriage, determining guardianship and legitimacy of children, negotiating inheritance and wills, establishing courts, and codifying laws. However, while religious boundaries had been activated within Lebanese society even before the civil war, Lebanon's civil war caused the salience of these boundaries to increase. The civil war generated social and political conditions wherein, when people are asked to choose between national and sect loyalties, loyalty to sect repeatedly wins.[3] This dynamic continues to be seen even in the twenty-first century, when national political conflicts inevitably organize around religious allegiances and strategic alliances among sect leaders.

Violence, the NGO Sector, and the Lebanese State

Whether collaborating with government or filling gaps in services created by the absence of the state, NGOs play a pivotal role in the provision of health and social services in the developing world. The same is true in Lebanon. Lebanon's civil war severely weakened the Lebanese state, and this near absence of state power has had the effect of increasing the strength of the NGO sector in Lebanon. Some have attributed this strength to the fact that a lack of state power means a lack of authoritarian efforts to curb the NGO sector, which has allowed the voluntary sector in Lebanon to flourish in comparison to other parts of the Arab world. According to this interpretation, Lebanon's flourishing NGO sector is not the result of the good will of the Lebanese government but results from its lack of ability to exert authoritarian control over associative activity.[4] Although the civil war and the resulting weakness of the Lebanese state was a recurring theme in interviews with NGO staff in Lebanon, one staff member, whom I will call Najib, attributed Lebanon's vibrant NGO sector not only to the weak state but also to Lebanon's comparatively liberal association laws. (Najib, and all other names used to identify persons interviewed here, have been arbitrarily assigned. Throughout this book, in order to protect the confidentiality of interview participants, no real names are used.)

> The economy, the diversity, the social fabric of Lebanon have been very encouraging and supportive of NGOs and associative activity and such, while in the neighboring countries you may not have that. Although our law of association goes back to the Ottomans to 1901, it still is more liberal than the association laws that were enacted in the neighboring countries in the 2000s, like in Egypt and Jordan and other places. The law is liberal, it doesn't require licensing, it just talks about participation. So all you have to do when you form an NGO is to inform the government so that you are not pursued by people accusing you of forming a secret association. So you just declare that you have established an NGO, you just send your incorporation bylaws, and the moment they are received if you have not broken any law you can start your work. It has been very, very liberal compared to other places.

However, much of the prominence of the NGO sector in Lebanon comes from its role in providing health and social services in the absence of the state. This is a role that began during the civil war and has persisted until the present, with NGOs being the predominant health and social service providers in the country. In some cases NGOs were created during the war period in order to provide services, but often pre-existing organizations shifted their activities in order to meet the needs of the war's victims. Michel explained how his NGO's focus on youth development and recreation shifted during the war. "When the war broke out in '75, [our NGO] had to decide to shift its activities, so [our NGO] shifted into relief, into emergency relief. No one cared about swimming any more, and anyway, the swimming pools were not even accessible.

At that point [our NGO] started to get involved in providing shelter, medicines, food for the victims of the war and for the displaced, because in that time people used to be displaced from their areas of location to other areas. So [our NGO] started getting involved in that."

NGOs' role of taking on tasks perceived as being the domain of the state increased their credibility with the Lebanese population, with staff members reporting that NGOs often are more trusted than the government. This gap-filling role has also brought the NGOs a certain amount of bargaining power with the state, as Wael described. "We have some power and respect now, because during the war the government was not there so the local NGOs were trying to fill in the gaps. They moved into areas that were supposed to be the domain of the government. When the government returned back or the situation changed, the NGOs said, 'Okay, you left us to face the catastrophe so we would like to capitalize on this, we don't want to just be treated as if the war is over so now we go home and now it's your job to do.'"

In spite of this increase in power, most staff members lamented the lack of state service provision, feeling that the degree of need is so overwhelming that they are unable to provide services of the quantity and quality they would prefer. Most suggested that the government should be strengthened so the NGO community can step aside and focus on smaller, more specific goals. These views were expressed even by workers from NGOs affiliated with the Shiite militant group Hezbollah, in spite of the fact that many claim Hezbollah aspires to become its own "state within a state." Hassan, an employee of an NGO operated by Hezbollah, noted,

> The first responsibility should be in the hand of the government. We are covering a stage, a period of time, where the government is weak. But once the government has full programs, and they are totally full, the government must cover all these services. Then we will become helpers rather than the original providers of service, the basic providers of service. We all hope and wish for that outcome. The gap is huge. Even though we try to complement each other with the other NGOs, the gap is very big. We have problems. So we are waiting for the government to start providing the services just so we can breathe.

The Role of Faith in Lebanese Social Service NGOs

Group loyalty often can be a motivator for altruistic behavior, and sometimes voluntary activity is characterized by an explicit focus on within-group giving and activities that benefit others who share a similar identity. Numerous studies of philanthropy indicate that charitable giving and the voluntary work of nonprofit organizations often target specific populations based on factors such as religion, race, ethnic or tribal identity, kinship ties, or national origin. Classical sociologists such as Weber and Durkheim recognized the role religious belief plays in motivating human behavior and giving rise to communal activity, and sociology of religion has been incorporated into theorizing on a number of subjects often associated with the nonprofit sector, including altruism, civic engagement, and civil society.[5]

Studies also show that religious congregations themselves often find faith, mission, and action in the community to be inextricably linked. Social action and community service often are justified by the values held by the congregation, and serving the local community is seen as an integral part of practicing one's faith. Indeed, supply-side theories of the nonprofit sector suggest that the emergence of nonprofit organizations has less to do with a demand for services than with the supply of entrepreneurs who are committed to the establishment of those services. These theorists suggest that one of the most likely sources of such entrepreneurs is religious institutions, particularly in circumstances where religious competition exists. Some argue that religious groups create nonprofit institutions not entirely because of altruistic intentions, but for the instrumental purpose of winning new adherents. The formation of NGOs is thus a way in which religious groups can win devotees to their religion, the goal being that those with a desperate need for education, health care, or other basic supports will come to accept the faith of those who sponsor such services.[6]

In Lebanon, as well as in Sri Lanka and Bosnia and Herzegovina (as will be discussed later in the book), group loyalty, religious ties, and religious faith all play an important role in service provision by faith-based nonprofits. Chapter 3 also will discuss the important role that a drive to recruit new religious adherents plays in the NGO sector in Sri Lanka, and the conflicts created by that drive. In Lebanon, NGO employees make the influence of group belonging and religious belief clear as they explain how they choose their career, the added benefits they believe faith brings to service provision, and their perception that faith itself is one of the services they provide.

Choosing to Work in an NGO: The Roles of Community and Faith

Much as religious identity and religious belief often are a motivation for charity and altruism more generally, research has shown that faith plays an important role in motivating the employees and volunteers of faith-based nonprofit service providers.[7] This proves to be true in Lebanon as well. More than two-thirds of all staff members interviewed in Lebanon indicated that their professional training and/or past professional experience in health and social services was one factor that led them to work for their NGO. However, personal ties within particular religious communities and spiritual belief and inspiration also played an important role in leading many staff members to work for their organization. The influence of group belonging and religious belief on career choice is particularly relevant when we consider the mechanisms of collective violence discussed in Chapter 1. If individuals are strongly influenced by their membership in a faith group or by the beliefs and practices of their religion when choosing a career, one would expect that religious identity is highly salient for those individuals. As was discussed in Chapter 1, theories of collective violence assert that in a context of past religious violence, identity salience should be high, boundaries between groups should be activated, and individuals should differentiate between interactions within and among religious groups. It is this process of boundary activation that creates the potential for exclusionary and socially damaging behavior by NGO staff.

Nearly half of all staff members interviewed in Lebanon mentioned that their personal ties within a particular religious community had led them to work for their NGO. These personal ties typically involved a member of their religious congregation informing them of the availability of a job and referring them to the individual responsible for hiring, or their own personal ties to the NGO due to previous volunteer work through their religious congregation. Staff members from Druze and Christian faith-based organizations (FBOs) were most likely to indicate that they had come to work for their organization as a consequence of personal ties they had within their religious community, whereas less than half as many staff members from Muslim FBOs mentioned that they had come to their job because of similar personal ties.

In addition to mentioning personal ties, a number of staff members explained how they came to work for their NGO with stories about religious belief and religious inspiration. Staff members from Christian FBOs were most likely to indicate that religious belief or religious inspiration was one of the factors that drew them to work for their organization, and they often indicated that they viewed social service provision as a type of religious ministry. The following quotations from Lena and Leila illustrate the role that religious belief plays in motivating staff members from Christian NGOs.

> We hope that this economic crisis would end someday, but again, even if it ends there will be families that will be in need of support, so actually, again as Christians our ministry is to help others. That's what we learn from our Lord and we try to apply it here as a church, both financially and sometimes in different other social ministries, in counseling, in guiding people.

> To us, we are just trying to reflect Christ's love to those needy people. We are just trying to tell them that God cares, that our Lord cares about them, and we are just trying to fulfill the ministry that is assigned to us.

However, Christians were not alone in seeing religious belief as a motivation for working in a social service NGO. More than half of staff members from Muslim FBOs stated that religious belief or inspiration was one of the factors that drew them to work for the organization. This was particularly the case among staff of NGOs operated by Hezbollah. Staff members from Shiite Muslim FBOs shared examples of Muslim teachings that emphasize the imperative of offering service to others. Ali and Hussein explain:

> We were living in areas that were poor, and the need for services motivated us and gave us incentives. What added to this is the religious and moral side, the *hadith* (religious teachings). There is a *hadith* that I still remember that says, "all the creatures are sons of God," so it described God as a man and all the creatures as his sons, "and the most close to God is he who is most beneficial," so God said he is the father of all and the closest one to him is the one that benefits people the most. So this is one example of a really expressive *hadith,* it explains the role of human beings, and the principal role of the human being is to serve other people. There are lot of *hadith* that explain that people ought to serve each other.

> ———

> The prophet said that he who sleeps and doesn't care about others is not a Muslim. So imagine, if I come here and I know that there is a sick man and I don't help him, then I am not a Muslim or a human.

No staff members from Druze organizations indicated that religious belief had played a role in leading them to their NGO work. This may be because, whereas Islam obliges its adherents to make charitable contributions of material goods and labor as a form of *zakat,* or alms giving, *zakat* took on a very different meaning when the Druze religion diverged from Islam some thousand years ago. For the Druze faithful, the donation of material goods or labor is not considered sufficient to satisfy the requirement of *zakat,* and therefore *zakat* in the material sense is seen as less important than the act of soul cleansing and purification.[8] In fact Soha, a staff member from a Druze FBO, explained *zakat* as a practice that falls entirely outside the Druze religion. "The Muslims have much more income than we do. They are much more in numbers, and they have their zakat. I don't know if you know about the zakat. It's an obligatory donation in the Muslim religion. To give zakat, especially in Ramadan, it's an obligation. They are obliged to give this, 2 percent of their income to charity. The Muslims have to give it, but the Druze don't have zakat, so we don't have to. It's up to your wish and up to your ability, if you can give or not."

Druze FBO staff members are undoubtedly engaged in charitable work, but their attitudes and behavior appear to be influenced more by humanitarian aims than by religious belief. It may seem counterintuitive that Druze staff did not mention being motivated by religious belief but, as was discussed earlier, were very likely to have found their NGO position through social networks in the Druze community. However, as will be seen later in the chapter, the Druze have a small community within which social networks play a very important role regardless of the degree to which one actively practices one's faith.

The Added Benefits of Faith

The question of whether religious identity influences how services are provided stands at the crux of the policy debate over faith-based initiatives in the United States and other countries in the global north. Those in favor of increasing support for faith-based service provision often assert that FBOs' services are more effective thanks to more caring, compassionate, and supportive methods used by staff members motivated by faith. International faith-based organizations working in developing countries sometimes are perceived as exhibiting greater long-term commitment to local communities than secular NGOs, an argument that is made about FBOs in the global north as well. Supporters of faith-based service provision also argue that services provided by religious organizations have moral and spiritual aspects that are desirable and that make them particularly well suited for working with populations with problems such as substance abuse, violence, and incarceration. Indeed, research demonstrates a strong positive correlation between engagement in religious behavior and increased health and well-being, although it remains to be determined whether religion causes individuals to choose healthful, positive behaviors, or whether other factors cause the same individual to engage in both healthful, positive behaviors and religious practice.[9]

However, the degree to which religious service provision is different from service provision by secular organizations is hotly debated, and opponents of faith-based service provision often note the lack of empirical evidence demonstrating that services provided by FBOs are more effective than those provided by secular organizations. There is a growing body of research demonstrating the effectiveness of faith-based service provision, but these studies regularly fail to examine a comparison group served by a secular organization, making it impossible to assess whether FBOs are *more* effective than other types of service providers. Some scholars even argue that although faith may indeed bring greater compassion, employees and volunteers of FBOs can be plagued by a certain "philanthropic amateurism" that prevents them from responding professionally to the true needs of community members. In spite of their good intentions, these workers instead seek to direct prayers and interventions toward a group of service recipients they have socially constructed as poor and undeveloped, and whose needs often are attributed to moral deficiencies. While such practices largely have fallen out of favor in northern countries as professionalism increasingly becomes the norm in the nonprofit sector, the developing world may be more susceptible to these approaches.[10] Because of these debates regarding the influence of faith on service provision, the idea that religious identity gives some form of added benefit to the services rendered by FBOs has been the topic of a great deal of research on the nonprofit sector.

Numerous staff members from Lebanese FBOs believed that their religious identity brought certain benefits to their organization. Aside from its pertinence to the debate discussed above, the presence of this belief is important analytically because it provides yet another indication of the salience of religion for FBO staff members. More than two-thirds of FBO staff felt that the religious orientation of their organization added value to the services they provide. The staff members who indicated that faith added benefits to their services included more than half of staff members from Muslim FBOs and all staff members from Christian FBOs. No participants from Druze FBOs and, perhaps obviously, no participants from secular NGOs indicated that faith added any value to the services they provide. The added benefits that staff members perceived faith as bringing to their organizations' work included

- added credibility in the community
- more individualized and compassionate service provision
- more highly committed and motivated workers
- greater safety for service recipients
- less conflict and greater trust among NGO staff

Several of these qualities are similar to those espoused by policymakers advocating faith-based service provision in the United States and other northern countries. Benefits such as individualized, compassionate service provision and committed, motivated workers frequently appear in literature on FBOs. However, some of the benefits mentioned by FBO staff in Lebanon, as well as by FBO staff in Sri Lanka and Bosnia and Herzegovina, as will be discussed in future chapters, are not discussed often in the global north. These benefits seem to be particularly significant for organizations operating in contexts of development.

Added Credibility
In the context of international development, sometimes faith-based nonprofits are seen as particularly desirable partners because of their intricate knowledge of local context and a shared religious solidarity with their service recipients. These organizations are often viewed as being more firmly embedded in local communities, and more trusted by locals, due to high levels of confidence in religious leaders. Even in the United States, FBOs are seen as having greater connection to and credibility within local communities because they are "home-grown" organizations whose staff members often have personal and family roots in local neighborhoods.[11] Along similar lines, staff members from Christian and Shiite

FBOs felt that the religious orientation of their NGO increased their credibility in their local community. No staff members from Druze or Sunni FBOs mentioned a relationship between faith and credibility. Almost a third of staff members believed that this positive perception in the community extended even to community members of other sects. Iskandar notes that although his organization is Christian, the religious nature of its work gives the organization added credibility even among non-Christians. "I have heard for example Muslim parents in the area who say that they prefer to send their children to our organization because they sense that there is the fear of God. Now, it's not that we are doing anything to them, but this is the sense, it is an atmosphere. Nothing, no specific substance, but they have a sense that it is a church owned thing and they feel safe. They feel that there are at least general morals, fairness, so that makes it effective."

More Individualized and
Compassionate Service Provision
Staff members from Christian FBOs also mentioned more individualized and compassionate service provision as one added benefit that came from their religious belief. As noted earlier, this is a common claim among supporters of faith-based service provision in the global north, although academic studies have provided varying degrees of support for it. International FBOs working in developing countries sometimes are perceived as exhibiting greater long-term commitment to local communities than secular NGOs, which is said to allow for greater individualized contact. Also, it is not unusual for Christian organizations in particular to couch their service provision as based in compassion, a notion that is central to Christian theology. The concept of compassion is also central to other faiths, such as Buddhism, which asserts that happiness comes as a result of one's compassionate words and acts.[12] Miriam describes how Christian faith causes her FBO to seek more individualized solutions to people's problems. "It is a very needs-based work that we do here. If someone comes in with a special need, let's say addiction, we don't just say, 'Sorry, we cannot help you.' Because we want to, as a Christian

organization, we want to go beyond services, we want to go beyond that, we want to help with the individual person's needs, of course within our limitations and our resources. It is a very needs-based service. Every family has its own needs."

Staff members from Christian FBOs also indicated that their faith caused them to have greater compassion toward service recipients, as Ghada notes. "For example for social work, approaching the person on the principles of Christian values I think is the basis of a lot of this. The social workers we have are committed Christians, so they depend on the Christian teaching. Now, they can be as categorical as non-Christians maybe, but the kindness that they show would be based on their Christian belief. Of course this has a very positive impact on the person receiving the aid."

However, particularly in the development literature, service driven by compassion does not come without criticism. In international development contexts, particularly when NGO workers are from a different country and of a different faith than community members, some suggest that faith and compassion do not necessarily lead to meaningful dialogue with community members about the causes and implications of their situation. Because in Christian theology compassion is often expressed by directing action toward an object of pity, some argue that this social construction of service recipients limits the degree to which meaningful and equal interaction can occur between the "helper" and the "helped." In addition, because some NGO workers assume that work fueled by compassion will automatically bring positive benefits, some organizations fail to assess the results of their work in a critical manner.[13]

More Motivated and Committed Workers

Another assertion often made in the United States context is that FBOs have more highly motivated workers and have access to a large pool of committed volunteers. Both Christian and Muslim staff members indicated that they believed religious faith caused their workers to be more committed in the face of adversity. Khalil noted that faith motivates the staff of his Christian FBO to continue their work in spite of the financial hardships the organization faces. "In no way can we justify keeping these programs open, because we do not make money from these services . . . we are in debt, we are hardly paying the salaries of the workers. And all this is not justified, if you look at it financially. It is a big headache! You should not keep such an institution open. But it is our faith that pushes us to work, and to work with great joy. I mean, at no point do we complain about all the difficulties. Yes, there are difficulties, and we will try to do our best, but we also believe that God blesses what we do, blesses others who walk with you, and so that's what keeps us going. It is because of our faith that we go on doing this."

Abdullah, a staff member of a Hezbollah-affiliated Muslim FBO, describes how religious faith causes workers from his organization to be more motivated and more willing to take risks on behalf of service recipients than other NGOs or the Lebanese government. "Let me tell you that for war we are always prepared and we are ready to move to help refugees and those who are injured. [One international NGO] cannot always go in when some areas are bombarded, but we go in, because the people who work here are so courageous that they do that. The people who work here do not work for salary, or for position, or for personal benefit. It's an internal commitment that is strong. We're highly motivated. Therefore, ten of us will produce more than one thousand civil servants, and we will be more committed because we have commitment to God, and to religion. I think this is a big difference."

Increased Safety for Service Recipients

In addition to benefits that have been noted in literature on faith-based nonprofit organizations in the global north, staff members from FBOs noted other benefits that they perceive religious belief offers to their organization. Some staff members from Christian FBOs noted that they think their religious identity provides greater safety for service recipients. This additional safety was attributed to the religious belief of workers, which staff members suggested ensured a protective and caring environment for service recipients. In addition, some staff members mentioned that the ability to check employees' backgrounds through Christian social networks provided a safer environment for service recipients as well. Jamil captured both of these ideas as he described the safe service environment within his NGO.

> Since most of the people who work here know that they are doing this for God, in this way I think it helps provide a safer environment for the children and maybe a more caring environment where they could enjoy love and security. Actually, we won't employ anybody here unless they come from a church with a recommendation from their pastor as a letter of reference. So that also helps keep track of people's past and gives you an idea of their backgrounds and if they have any serious problems in their past. So in this way I think since most of the people who work here come from a Christian background, that helps the organization make sure that the children are in safe hands.

Less Conflict and
Greater Trust Among Staff

Staff members from both Christian and Muslim FBOs indicated that they believe the faith orientation of their organization results in less conflict and greater trust among workers in the organization. This is attributed to an increased sense of team spirit and mutual trust, as well as to having more aligned goals within the organization. "I think one of the key things about being a Christian organization is that all of our staff are practicing Christians and I think that fosters a much better environment, there is very much a team spirit and a sense of people supporting one another, praying for one another. Staff relationships, I'm not saying there aren't tensions from time to time, but generally staff relationships are very good and I think that reflects in people's work." Ahmed, a staff member from a Muslim organization, expresses similar feelings: "Because of our religion there is trust among our group and our members and this gives us more power. We also have aligned goals, and we are very organized, which provides us power. We don't have lots of internal conflict within the organization, even though we have participation in decision making on all levels."

Religion as a Service Rendered

An interesting pattern that came to light during interviews with FBO staff is that religion not only was perceived by staff members as adding value to the services they provided but also was portrayed as service itself within their portfolio of offerings. Over one-third of staff members, all from Christian FBOs, described religion as a service offered to clients. In some cases, explicitly religious activities such as Bible lessons were described as one of the services offered, as the following comments illustrate.

> At the moment half of the children we serve are Christians, and half are Muslims, roughly. But all of them enjoy or profit from the same services, including the spiritual programs. They all participate in all the programs that we have.

> ———

> We are a Christian organization, and we make that clear right from the very beginning. So when we have an interview, when we meet the child's family, we will say right from the word go that we are a Christian organization, and as part of the services we offer we teach the Bible, and families have to sign an agreement saying that they accept that and agree with that.

In addition to concrete religious activities, other staff members from Christian FBOs describe the more informal spiritual guidance, religious teachings, and emotional support they offer as an important part of their work and a means of offering help to service recipients. As Rana and Josie explain,

> Anyone, any elderly or any child or teenager who hears something about God and what the Bible says, they would feel more or less

relieved. So that is one way of helping the person, to help them have a different type of hope than what the surroundings will give. This is what makes our work different. The other services we give, the medical and financial services, these are similar to other institutions. Only the message of God is what makes our work different, and the way we give it to children and teenagers and elderly. Sometimes nothing that we can say can make things easy for the other individual, but when we give them the Bible and then try to say something, that makes his day better. That's how we try to help.

Our aim is not only to educate people so they can make a good life, but to show them that life is worth living. I believe that we as people of faith would like people to see that it is not only by money or by material things that people live their life, but to show them that God has a purpose for their life and finding that purpose makes life meaningful. This is something we can give them.

Depictions of religious activities as simply an additional item in one's portfolio of services were unique to staff from Christian FBOs, as were stories about sharing faith in the process of other social service activities. Perhaps this is not surprising, given that Christian belief, though very diverse among Christianity's various denominations, takes a holistic view of development and often considers spiritual deprivation just as damaging as material deprivation. In development practice Christianity employs theologies of economic salvation and spiritual salvation, so serving the poor is an activity that involves both the body and the spirit.[14] As Rima puts it, "Basically, we view our services in two categories: financial, and that's relief, and developmental, which includes Christian education. That's where reaching out to the individuals spiritually takes place."

It is important to note that no staff from Christian FBOs or other FBOs explicitly mentioned a goal of recruiting adherents to their religion, even though this is sometimes discussed as one possible goal of faith-based social service providers.[15] However, more than 75 percent of staff from Christian FBOs mentioned that sharing their religious beliefs, religious teachings, or the "word of God" with individuals receiving services was one goal of their organization's work. As Fillipe explains, "I do believe, as Christians we believe that we provide here for those children the opportunity to hear the message of the gospel, and that is very important for us. Another main message for us is to provide a good educational program for those children. . . . So the spiritual program and then the educational program, our priorities go like this."

In other contexts FBO staff members are more explicit about their goal of proselytization, and evangelic activities create a great deal of social and political tension in local communities. Chapter 3 will describe the case of Sri Lanka, where both actual evangelism and a fear of evangelism have caused tremendous conflict that has risen to the level of national political debate.

Sectarianism and Service Provision

Interviews with staff members of both FBOs and secular NGOs indicate that in Lebanon, NGO social service provision is quite clearly structured along sectarian lines. All staff members from Druze, Shiite, and Sunni FBOs indicated that between 95 and 100 percent of the people their organization serves come from their own sect. Although staff members from Christian FBOs more often reported serving a group that comprised individuals of different religions, more than half still indicated that their services primarily benefited other Christians.

Scholars of Lebanon's social structure note that religious sects are politically significant because of their role in enhancing personal and group security for the Lebanese population.[16] In a context of sectarian warfare, belonging to a sect that has the resources to protect one's family from physical harm is of obvious consequence. This sectarian provision of security also extends to the economic and human security offered by social service organizations. Indeed, most staff members attributed the sectarian patterns of their NGO's service provision to the inherently sectarian nature of service provision in Lebanon. As Mansoor, a staff member from a Sunni Muslim FBO, notes,

It's not in our rules or regulations to accept only Muslim children, but we have to be realistic. I mean, this is Lebanon. Lebanon is divided. We don't reject any child because of their religion, but this is the situation everywhere. I mean, if you go to the Druze (NGOs), you will see that the majority are Druze. If you go to the Shiite foundations, you see that most are Shiites. If you go to the Christian (NGOs), you will see that they are Christian. I am sure it is also not in their rules or regulations, but the environment of Lebanon, it is a mosaic country, and with the geographical distribution, and with the sect lists, this is the normal situation. But we do not have any rule about it. On the contrary, we would like to have children with different religions. But on the ground if you come to visit us you will see that most are Muslims, Muslims of all sects. If you go to Christians you will see that most are Christians, and if you go to Druze you will see that most are Druze.

Afifi, a staff member from a Druze FBO, notes the same phenomenon and attributes it to the behavior of service recipients, who she says prefer to approach organizations from their own sect. "We don't make a difference [among religions when providing services]. Everybody who asks, we give. But mainly, mainly Druze. Because Muslims have their own organizations, so they go to their own organization. Christians have their own organizations, so they go to their own organization. But we never say no to anybody."

Rashid, a staff member from a Hezbollah-affiliated Shiite FBO, mentioned how geographic segregation in terms of religion and political affiliation influences where his FBO can provide services. "Mostly our services target the areas where mostly Shiites live. The people who benefit are not always Shiites; they might be Shiites, but if the areas they live in are mixed, you might have Christians, you might have Sunnis, and you have Shiites who benefit from the services. Because we are considered part of Hezbollah and the resistance, it is not easy. Because we are considered Hezbollah, it is not easy for us to provide services in an area that is dominated by another sect, because this might be seen as infringing on the other sect, and they would not be happy [laughs]. So even if we wanted to, we are not trying."

Some staff members offered more specific reasons for sectarian divisions in service provision, including language barriers in service provision and the desire to preserve ethnic identity. However, these specific reasons were mentioned only by staff members from Armenian and Palestinian NGOs. The specific case of Armenian and Palestinian NGOs will be discussed later in this chapter.

Openness to Other Sects

In spite of the clearly sectarian structure of service provision by FBOs, none of the FBO staff members explicitly stated that religious sect was a criterion they considered when selecting service recipients. Poverty was an important criterion applied by many NGOs; it was mentioned by all staff members from Druze, Shiite, and Sunni NGOs, by more than 85 percent of staff members from Christian FBOs, and by more than 50 percent of staff members from secular NGOs. All staff members indicated that some specific tangible need served as a criterion by which they select which individuals they will serve. Examples include having a specific medical condition or disability and being a victim of domestic abuse (in either case, regardless of income).

In fact, in spite of reporting that they serve primarily members of their own sect, all of the staff members from Sunni, Shiite, and Druze FBOs explicitly stated that their organization was willing to serve people of other sects and would not turn away people from other sects who asked for services. In contrast, less than 45 percent of staff members from Christian FBOs made similar statements. Staff members were not asked a direct question about their openness to serving individuals from other sects, so this could reflect the fact that, having already indicated that they serve a mixed population, participants from Christian FBOs felt less compelled to emphasize their openness to serving others.

Many staff members from Sunni, Shiite, and Druze FBOs made a point of giving examples of times when they had served someone of another sect in an apparent effort to demonstrate their openness to service recipients from other groups. One interesting example is a story proudly told by a staff member from a Palestinian NGO regarding an incident when they had provided health care to an Israeli soldier. "We don't differentiate between Muslim, Christian, Jewish—it is a humanitarian organization, so we should receive the patients and treat the patients. I remember, during the Israeli invasion in 1982, we had one of the injured soldiers who was captured. He was in our clinic and he was Jewish, and we treated him and we gave him afterward to the Israelis. So we didn't differentiate, to us he was just injured. We didn't differentiate [on the basis of] race, color, religion, nationality. We are working as humanitarians."

In addition to those who offered examples of the few instances when they had served individuals from other sects, some staff members gave specific reasons why they made efforts to serve people outside their own sect. These reasons included professionalism in service provision, the inclusive nature of their religious teachings, and concerted efforts to promote cross-cultural understanding.

Professionalism in Service Provision
One reason that staff members offered for making an effort to serve people outside their own sect was the professional nature of their service provision. Fares, a staff member from a Hezbollah-affiliated Shiite FBO, describes the professional, needs-based manner in which his organization selects service recipients. "The most important element in this institution is that we don't have any conditions, so we won't care about religion, your political affiliation, or your dress code, all that we care about is that you need a loan. Our health institutions have centers, like clinics, or health centers, or emergency centers, and these institutions have the same general policy, their services are open to anyone. Any sick person could be accepted and these institutions are open to all religions."

Abdo, a staff member from a Christian FBO, explains how this professionalism has helped his organization gain trust in communities dominated by other sects.

> Our motto is that we do not ask you what sect you are from. Now, definitely acceptance doesn't come easily. It takes two or three years

of commitment, of being there, of being value-oriented and not religion-oriented, being with the people and in partnership with the people, of listening to them and caring for them and deciding with them what to do rather than just coming in with our own ideas. Now, in that sense, people in Muslim villages, in fundamentalist areas, even in Hezbollah villages, they are aware of [our NGO] and our work, and they don't object to that. We work in certain villages where Hezbollah has a presence and they respect our work and they don't see us as a threat, and we still manage to promote and make visible our identity as a value-oriented organization.

Inclusive Nature of Religious Teachings

Several staff members from Muslim FBOs offered the inclusiveness of the Muslim religion as a reason to be open to people of other sects. These staff members gave examples of teachings from Islam to explain why they would be open to serving people of other sects, even if in practice they serve primarily Muslims.

> We believe as Muslims that we are also Jews, and we are Christians, and then we are Muslims, because we believe the Jewish religion, we agree with all teachings of the Jewish religion. Also, we agree with all the teachings of the Christian religion, and we believe all that came after that with the Prophet Muhammad, peace be upon him. So, any Muslim, if he is a real Muslim, he has to be compassionate with all people, whether they are Jewish, or—now, I am not talking politics. I am talking about human beings. A Muslim has to be compassionate with all of them. So if a person is in need we have to help him, even if he is Christian, if he is any religion, if we are truly implementing the Muslim religion. So any person who comes here, if this person needs help, we see if we can help him within our ability.

> Imam Ali was one of the famous figures after the prophet, and he said people are either brothers in religion or peers in creation. So you should interact with them justly and in the same way because it doesn't matter what is the religion. Not the skin color, not the region, or tribe, or religion. Humanity is the highest point. So there are a number of

lessons from the prophet—he referred to this one thing but there are a number of them.

Concerted Efforts to Promote Cross-Cultural Understanding

In a few instances, staff members from Christian FBOs indicated that they served people from different sects in a concerted effort to promote understanding and tolerance between the different groups in Lebanese society. Jad noted, "In Lebanon all they do is competing, different groups competing with the others. I have these rights so they should have these rights, or they got this so I need an equal thing, and so on. I said, 'This is not the way we work at [our NGO]. It's a place where you learn to appreciate the other. You don't need to be like them, but you learn to appreciate. You learn about them, you learn from them, with them.'"

Sevag, a staff member from an Armenian Christian FBO, noted that although his organization provides services to all sects because of the broad educational and training goals of the institution, he also believes an added value comes from cultural exchange.

"Because we are owned by an ethnic group, a small ethnic group, which in an Arab context is Armenian, then suddenly you realize there is a cultural agenda. Cultural exchange. And lots of people, lots of Armenians, for the first time in their life, sit next to non-Armenians, that close every day. And for lots of Arabs, it's the first time that they sit next to these people that speak Armenian. The same would be true about Christians and Muslims. There's some who come to our institution and sit next to people who are not Christian for the first time. And also true about the Muslims. So I realize that there is a mission that is bigger than education and training, which we cherish, and which we focus on."

Inclusive in Theory, Sectarian in Practice

If NGO workers indeed are open to serving members of other sects, why is service provision so clearly divided along religious lines? As Afifi from the Druze FBO noted earlier, one possibility is that even though staff members may be more than happy to serve people from other sects, potential service recipients may be reluctant to seek services from NGOs of other sects because of the history of violence and the highly activated boundaries that exist between Lebanon's religious groups. This question can be truly answered only by gathering information from potential service recipients, but Kareem, a staff member from a Sunni FBO, suggested this might be the case. "I think this is only natural that people might first approach people from their own religion. I mean, if I have a problem, the first person I go to, I go to my family. If my family cannot help me then I go to my friends. If my friends cannot help me then I try to approach someone else."

However, the fact that the majority of staff members from *secular* NGOs also indicated that they primarily served individuals from a single sect suggests that geographic segregation is also an important factor. There are no accurate census data available that can illuminate the degree of geographic segregation that exists in Lebanon, but most agree that the country is segregated on the basis of sect. In daily life the Lebanese often can accurately ascertain an individual's sect membership merely by knowing the village or neighborhood in which that individual lives. Even though I was a foreign researcher from the United States, Lebanese from all sects quickly guessed the sect of my Lebanese hosts simply from the names of the villages I had visited as a tourist. If service recipients seek services primarily in the communities where they live, and if these communities are segregated along religious lines, this would explain why even service recipients from secular NGOs tend to be predominantly from a single sect. As Nadia, a staff member from a secular NGO, noted, "Our students are mainly Sunni due to the geographic area where the center is located, but our staff are mixed."

The Separation and Intersection of Ethnicity and Religion

In addition to interviewing staff from FBOs of Lebanon's various religious groups, I also spoke with staff of faith-based and secular NGOs serving the Armenian and Palestinian communities in Lebanon. These organizations reported the same sectarian pattern in service provision that other organizations reported, and these patterns in service provision are probably affected by many of the same factors that affect other NGOs. However, staff from Armenian and Palestinian NGOs reported motivations for service provision that were much different from those reported by other NGOs and FBOs. Both minorities have been influenced by their past experiences of violence or exclusion, and this has led to very high identity salience for NGO staff members. However, whereas religion seems to intersect with ethnic identity as a motivation for Armenian staff members, Palestinian staff members carefully distanced themselves from religion, instead embracing their national identity.

One Nation Under God—The Armenians in Lebanon

During the First World War, 1.5 million Armenians were killed in what was then Turkish Armenia. During this period the Turks attempted to extinguish the Armenians in the Armenian provinces of the Ottoman Empire through systematic ethnic cleansing. Although the genocide has been carefully documented, it remains categorically denied by the Turkish government. Thousands of Armenians who were fleeing the massacres and deportation found sanctuary in Lebanon, where they were legally integrated into Lebanese society. As of 1998, Armenians in Lebanon numbered around 150,000.[17]

Armenian political parties played some supportive roles in the disputes of the civil war, but they were not directly involved in the conflict. Therefore, the religious divisions of the civil war seem to have little influence on the sense of identity of Armenian staff members. As Aram noted, "No one really knew what to do with us during the civil war. The Christians assumed that because we are Christians we should be their natural ally, but we refused to side with them and the things they did. So the Christians hated us, which made the Muslims like us more. But they were so busy with each other that they left us out of things for the most part."

The Armenian population in Lebanon is predominantly Christian, and faith plays a strong role in the community. As Hairig explains,

"When you say Armenian you automatically mean Christian. Of course you have Armenians who have been converts to other religions, and you have those who are only nominally Christians, but no one usually says, 'I'm not a Christian.' When you say 'Armenian,' that's automatically Christian."

However, in spite of the strong salience of their Christian identity, it is not the violence of the Lebanese civil war that influences Armenian staff members, but the violence and exclusion of the Armenian genocide and mass deportation. Without fail, all staff members from Armenian NGOs discussed the genocide and how it influenced their work. The historical experience of the Armenian genocide often intersected with Christian faith as a motivation and inspiration for service provision, a congruence captured by Nareg:

> If you know anything about the genocide you know that about 1.5 million Armenians were massacred, and the remnants of those people ran away and came to Syria and Lebanon. . . . But in that very very bad condition, the first thing they did was to establish schools and churches. I mean, they weren't people who nagged about their condition. Of course, a lot of help came from different countries and organizations, and we are very thankful for that. But in addition to that help, the Armenian people were convinced that education, that faith, came first. Their condition did not define their future. They defined the future through what they saw as very important, and that makes this work we do today very important. I mean, people had hopes that brought us up to this stage where we are today. So we cannot just forget schools and churches and social institutions just because of financial difficulties, just because we are in a bad position nowadays. This does not justify anything. We should keep on going as we have always done. We have seen far worse days than these days so this drives us to keep going, and this is something I am proud of as Armenian. And I hope that the coming generations will be as proud as our ancestors were in the old days.

Staff members from Armenian NGOs indicated that their organizations provided services almost exclusively to Armenians. Most staff members attributed this ethnically based service provision to the geographic segregation of their community and to linguistic barriers present for Arabic-speaking Lebanese in an Armenian language environment. Oshin mentions both of these as reasons why services are limited to Armenians. "The people we help are Armenian because the programs are in a neighborhood that is mostly populated by Armenians, and also the volunteers that work with the youth group and the playground, they are from our [Armenian] churches and our youth group, they volunteer to come and help work with the children, of course under the supervision of the social worker or the special counselor. So it's more of a linguistic thing than anything else."

However, a second reason for ethnically based service provision mentioned by some staff members was a desire to preserve the Armenian identity, language, and culture. Some perceived that this could be done only by keeping certain aspects of life, such as service provision, separate from mainstream Lebanese society. "But sadly, and I am speaking as an Armenian, we Armenians need to keep our identity. To do that we usually separate ourselves at least in some areas of life, because we have seen genocide, we know the danger of being dissolved or being canceled from the map, being lost forever. We have tasted that, and now we don't want a cultural genocide where Armenians will eventually become in Lebanon Lebanese, in Syria Syrians, in America Americans, and forget their language, culture, music, which is very rich."

Thus in the case of staff members from Armenian NGOs, ethnic identity and religious identity intertwine to influence the attitudes and behavior of NGO staff. The result of this high identity salience and its subsequent impact on behavior is the same as for other FBOs in Lebanon. Service provision becomes exclusive and structured along ethnic lines.

Choosing Nation over God—The Palestinians in Lebanon

After the 1948 defeat of the Arab armies by the Israelis, more than 750,000 Palestinians fled to neighboring Arab countries, and 200,000 settled in United Nations–operated camps near Lebanon's major cities.

Additional Palestinian refugees arrived after the 1967 Arab-Israeli war and Palestinian clashes in Jordan in 1970, bringing with them the Palestinian Liberation Organization infrastructure. Lebanon previously had welcomed refugees of Kurdish, Assyrian, and Armenian descent and had legally and socially integrated them into society, but the same was not true for the Palestinians. This was due in part to a broadly held belief among Arab countries that permanent integration would compromise the goal of Palestinian refugees ultimately returning to their homeland. In Lebanon an additional factor was the fear that integrating the Palestinians as a large group of mainly Muslim citizens would upset the country's religious political balance.[18] Many Palestinians continue to live segregated from the rest of Lebanese society in refugee camps, and they continue to face a number of legal and social barriers to their participation in Lebanese society.

Unlike the Armenians, Palestinians were highly affected by the Lebanese civil war. Growing power within Palestinian political institutions and military bases inside the refugee camps is one of the factors that fueled conflicts between Maronite Christians and Muslims and exacerbated the subsequent civil war. In addition, many of the massacres of the civil war were committed by Maronite Christian militias against non-Lebanese minorities, including Kurds, Syrians, and (most frequently) Palestinians.[19]

Considering the past and current living conditions of Palestinians in Lebanon, one can see at least three ways in which violence and exclusion might increase their identity salience. The establishment of the state of Israel, which pushed large numbers of Palestinians away from their land and into refugee communities throughout the Arab world, is a major factor that increases the salience of Palestinian national identity. The continual exclusion of Palestinian refugees from Lebanese society is a second factor that increases identity salience. A third factor is the violence Palestinians experienced during the Lebanese civil war. The staff members from Palestinian NGOs told stories indicating that all three of these factors had influenced their attitudes about the work in which their organizations were engaged. Their Palestinian identity salience was high, and all participants indicated that their Palestinian identity had far greater influence on their work than their religious identity.

Perhaps the most commonly mentioned complaint among Palestinian staff members was the exclusion of Palestinians from participation in Lebanese society. NGO workers saw this exclusion as having a negative impact on the practical nature of their work and as increasing their workload in many ways. Because Palestinians are forbidden by law from working in approximately seventy different professions, because they cannot be treated in Lebanese government hospitals, and because many are living in poor conditions in refugee camps, NGO workers felt that the social, economic, and health problems of service recipients were exacerbated. Tariq notes, "The Palestinians in Lebanon are forbidden from civil and human rights. We are not allowed to be treated in Lebanese government hospitals. About seventy-two types of jobs, we are not allowed to work in them. We are not allowed to inherit property, like if it's left to our children. . . . If you visit the camps you can see how they suffer from segregation, from health, the living conditions, from crowdedness of houses and crowdedness inside the houses, and we have a high percentage of chronic diseases."

Much like the Armenians, Palestinians have responded to the experience of being pushed out of their homeland by placing great importance on efforts to preserve their culture and identity. Staff members from Palestinian NGOs echo this conviction. Ibtihal explains, "One of our most important projects is saving the Palestinian heritage, the needlework and the embroidery that they do, the Palestinian folk dances. . . . We also have a project where we emphasize having every child know where he is from in Palestine, what city or village in Palestine, just to keep their memory."

Just as all Armenian NGO workers recounted stories of the Armenian genocide and their deportation from their homeland, all Palestinian NGO workers made reference to the massacre of Sabra and Shatila in Beirut in 1982. This massacre of well over 1,000 unarmed civilians took place in a Palestinian refugee camp in Beirut, and it has been blamed on both the Israeli Army and Christian militias.[20] The staff members from

Palestinian NGOs seemed less concerned with assigning blame and more interested in how the events had influenced the historical development of their organizations.

> We used to work in very hard, very, very harsh circumstances, and of course after the massacre we suffered at Shatila it got even worse and worse and more and more children and families needed help and sponsorship. So, then came the next war, what they call it is the civil or the camp wars, and of course every time, the problems are more and more. We needed more NGOs on the ground working with the children. And a lot of people, they were refugees. I mean, they are refugees in the camps, but because of the massacre they had to be refugees in other places too. They were evicted from camps, and they had to live here in [this neighborhood] and in the hills and deserted buildings. And at the same time they had people moving into the other camps. The problem with the Palestinians, it's like it is growing bigger each time with each problem.

One interesting characteristic of the interviews with the Palestinian NGO workers is their rejection of any affiliation with a religious identity. This usually came out in response to questions confirming that the NGO was not a faith-based organization. Several respondents took great care to explain that their Palestinian identity was most important, regardless of their religious identity.

> For the Palestinians, we feel that it doesn't really matter if we are Christians, if we are Druze, if we are Muslims, if we're Jews. We don't care, we are just Palestinians, you know? We are all Palestinians regardless of our religion. This is how I feel and this is how I feel that the Palestinians feel. Like here as I told you we have Christians and Muslims, and we live really peacefully, we are a family. And we have another camp, I don't know if you know about the other camp, it's Palestinian Christians there. You know, it's amazing, they still have the accent, the Palestinian accent. And for me, I'm a Muslim, but when I go there, I feel like I am going to Palestine. It's overwhelming for me just to be there. And I don't care—this is how we feel, the Palestinians. It's Palestine, it's Palestinians, it's not what your religion is.

Just as is true of the staff members from Armenian NGOs, ethnic identity has a strong influence on the attitudes and behavior of Palestinian NGO staff. And like the Armenian NGOs, the Palestinian NGOs serve almost exclusively recipients who share their ethnic identity. Most staff members attributed this to the geographic location of their work, which was typically focused inside Palestinian refugee camps. As is the case with the other NGOs examined, service provision is structured along identity-based lines.

Included or Excluded?
Religious Identity and Access to Services

Interviews with staff members indicate that access to NGOs' social services is structured in a manner that duplicates the existing religious and ethnic divisions in Lebanese society. Staff members from FBOs and from Armenian and Palestinian NGOs reported very high levels of identity salience and, in some cases, explicitly drew the connection between their strong identity and their past experiences of violence and exclusion. This awareness of identity and of across-boundary interactions influences the behavior not only of staff members but also presumably of service recipients, who may be reluctant to approach NGOs of other sects for assistance. The sectarian nature of service provision in Lebanon is further reinforced by geographic segregation, which leads even secular organizations to serve primarily members of a single sect.

Another factor that strengthens the sectarian nature of service provision and service access in Lebanon is reliance on service referrals from other religiously (or ethnically) identified organizations and from religious leaders. Religious referrals were one means by which many NGOs selected whom they would serve. In particular, 75 percent of staff members from Sunni FBOs and more than 85 percent of staff members from Christian FBOs used referrals from religious leaders or religious bodies as one way of selecting clients for services. As individuals approach religious or other community leaders for assistance, it is easy to imagine that these leaders first refer them to NGOs of the same religious (or ethnic) identity for services.

This certainly seems to be the case for one Druze FBO. Social networks within the Druze community are so tight that the FBO has preexisting information regarding who needs services. As Afifi explains, "Sometimes they come, they come and say [they need services], but we have our own statistics. You know, we [Druze] are a small community here. We are not a big community; actually lots of us know each other. So when they tell us they need this, we know if they really need services or not."

In spite of the fact that NGO staff members report collaboration with other members of the NGO community, including FBOs of other faiths, staff members from FBOs were much more likely to report cooperating with FBOs of the same faith than with FBOs of other faiths. The fact that even relationships among NGOs are structured along sectarian lines undoubtedly helps dictate where service recipients are referred when one NGO cannot meet their specific needs.

Lebanon's sectarian social service environment provides a perfect context for exclusion from services, particularly when service providers from certain sects are the sole service providers in their community. As was previously mentioned, the near absence of the Lebanese state in health and social service provision means that these fields have become the domain of Lebanon's NGO sector. There is a community of secular NGO service providers, but staff members indicate that secular NGOs usually target very specific needs, such as the needs of those with a specific disability or medical condition, rather than the more general needs of low-income communities. Indeed, staff members from secular NGOs were less likely than those from FBOs to report poverty as a criterion used when selecting service recipients. For the time being, it seems that much community-based health and social service provision that targets the poor remains in the hands of religious institutions and FBOs, who primarily serve members of their own sect.

Relative Capacity as Service Providers

But does sectarian service provision matter in the lives of the poor? The fact that service provision is structured along sectarian lines may pose little threat of exclusion from services, so long as all individuals have adequate access to the resources held within their particular sect and so long as all sects are equally equipped to provide the services that their sect members need. However, capacity for service provision and quality of services may differ substantially among sects. In assessing the relative access that members of different communities may have to basic services, one must consider the comparative capacity of different sects to provide services to their community. Smaller sects, such as the Druze and the smaller Christian minorities, often have less capacity to provide services than some of the larger and better-funded Shiite and Sunni institutions. Several staff members discussed their relative disadvantage as service providers when compared to other sects. As indicated earlier in this chapter, one staff member from a Druze FBO noted that the Muslims have greater financial capacity because of the tradition of *zakat*. As Alliyah, a staff member from a small Christian FBO, notes, "See, we are very, very small. They are very, very big. If you speak about the Catholic Church, their social work is huge. Of course, it depends on the number of population they have around here. The Islamic organizations are huge, they have a lot of financial possibilities, a lot of personnel possibilities. For example, the Greek Orthodox community here in Lebanon has a huge hospital. But we're not that big."

It does seem that when one sect has a comparative advantage in providing services, there are instances when institutions from different sects cooperate. Several individuals told stories of cooperative relationships they have with NGOs from different sects, but these stories were usually about collaboration between two or more well-equipped FBOs operating initiatives on a national scale. In contrast, Soha, a staff member from a Druze FBO, explained how they are assisted by larger Muslim organizations. "Mostly we are the only ones who serve the Druze.

But for example in [a Sunni orphanage], I think we have Druze in [the Sunni orphanage]. And in [a Muslim hospital], a hospital for elderly people who cannot move or care for themselves, I think we have about fifty Druze people there. So we always help them in Ramadan, we always either give them money or we take them food, like rice, sugar, such things. We take it to the Muslims, because we also have people there that they are caring for."

Rawan, a staff member from a well-financed Sunni FBO, described circumstances when individuals seeking services will approach another sect for services simply out of sheer need.

> In truth each sect provides services to its own community, so our services are mainly provided to Sunnis, with some exceptions. But for some of our specialized services people from other sects will approach our organization because their own sect does not provide them. When you provide so many services like we do then people of all religions come for services, because it is closer for them if their sect does not provide a specific service in their particular community, or if their sect does not provide that service at all.

Sole Service Provision by FBOs

As we noted in Chapter 1, the prevalence of service provision by a single NGO in much of the developing world further complicates the dynamics of access to services by poor individuals. In countries in the global north, where nonprofit organizations are heavily involved in the delivery of health and social services, it is usually reasonable to assume that service recipients are assisted by multiple public and nonprofit agencies, be it simultaneously or sequentially. However, this often is not the case in the developing world, where nonprofit organizations may virtually replace the state as service providers, and a single nonprofit organization is more likely to be the sole provider of a service in a particular community. Because service recipients' power within a service environment is directly dependent on their ability to access the same services from another provider, sole service provision places poor individuals in a position of tremendous dependence on the organization providing services. Poor individuals may have few if any resources to meet their basic needs if a sole service provider refuses to serve them based on their religion or ethnicity, if they are reluctant to approach the organization for services because of a history of violence and exclusion, or if they are simply unaware that the organization's services exist.[21]

All staff members from FBOs in Lebanon stated that other NGOs provide services that are similar to the services their organization provides, and more than half of staff members from secular NGOs stated that other NGOs provide similar services. However, a number of staff members from Christian, Shiite, and Sunni FBOs as well as from secular NGOs indicated that they were the sole providers of at least some services in some communities where they work. In addition, several staff members indicated that although their NGO might not be the sole service provider in a community, the services they provided were different in important ways from those provided by other NGOs. Examples included providing services at no or low cost, the organization's specific focus on a particular underserved community, the scope or sophistication of services, and the ways in which services were provided.

It is important to take into account that, depending on the level of cooperation an organization has with other NGOs in the community, staff members may not have an accurate sense of what services are provided by other NGOs, particularly NGOs from other religious sects. Nonetheless, the reported prevalence of sole service provision in Lebanon, combined with knowledge of the sectarian structure of NGO service provision, implies significant risk that access to service is lacking in some communities. This is particularly the case for those sects that may not have the capacity to provide sufficient services in all the communities where their members reside. The fact that most NGO staff report that they do not intentionally exclude clients based on sect bodes well for the ability of poor Lebanese to access services, as do stories of cooperation among different sects in service provision. These also bode well for the success of some of the practical solutions that are posed in Chapter 5. However, sectarian exclusion from services seems to be a strong possibility in Lebanon. The implications of leaving specific religious groups' human needs unmet must be weighed carefully in a society where relationships among sects remain delicate and resentment about the relative power and resources of different sects is high.

Notes

1. One scholar who discusses the sophisticated nature of Lebanon's nonprofit sector is Marzouk. See Mohsen Marzouk, "The Associative Phenomenon in the Arab World: Engine of Democratization or Witness to the Crisis?" in *NGOs, States and Donors: Too Close for Comfort?* ed. David Hulme and Michael Edwards (London: Macmillan Press, 1997): 191–201.

2. Numerous accounts of Lebanon's civil war have been published since the 1970s, many focusing on the political, economic, foreign relations, and military aspects of the civil war. However, in this section I rely rather heavily on Michael Johnson, *All Honourable Men: The Social Origins of War in Lebanon* (London: I. B. Tauris, 2002); and Latif Abul-Husn, *The Lebanese Conflict: Looking Inward* (Boulder, CO: Lynne Rienner Publishers, 1998). These authors focus specifically on the role that social conditions, social cleavages, and ethnic and religious identity played in the conflict, perspectives that are particularly relevant to my examination.

3. For more information see Abul-Husn, 1998; Johnson, 2002; and Elizabeth Picard, *Lebanon: A Shattered Country* (New York: Holmes & Meier, 2002).

4. For more on the relative strength of Lebanese and Palestinian civil society in comparison to other Arab countries, see Marzouk, 1997.

5. For more on the role of group loyalty in philanthropy, see Bradford Smith, Sylvia Shue, Jennifer Lisa Vest, and Joseph Villarreal,

Philanthropy in Communities of Color (Bloomington: Indiana University Press, 1999); and Robert Wuthnow, "Altruism and Sociological Theory," *Social Service Review* 67, no. 3 (1993): 344–58. For more on the role of religious belief in communal problem solving, see Émile Durkheim, *The Elementary Forms of the Religious Life* (New York: The Free Press, 1954); Warren F. Ilchman, Stanley Katz, and Edward L. Queen II, *Philanthropy in the World's Traditions* (Bloomington: Indiana University Press, 1998); and Max Weber, *The Sociology of Religion* (Boston, MA: Beacon Press, 1963).

6. For more on ties between community service and the practice of faith, see John P. Bartkowski, *The Promise and Peril of Charitable Choice: Faith-Based Initiatives in Mississippi* (Cambridge, MA: Harvard University Press, 2001); and Thomas Jeavons, *When the Bottom Line Is Faithfulness: Management of Christian Service Organizations* (Bloomington: Indiana University Press, 1994). For more information on supply-side theories of the nonprofit sector, see Estelle James, *The Nonprofit Sector in International Perspective: Studies in Comparative Culture and Policy* (New York: Oxford University Press, 1989). For more on nonprofit organizations as a tool for recruiting religious adherents, see Susan Rose-Ackerman, "Altruism, Nonprofits and Economic Theory," *Journal of Economic Literature* 34, no. 2 (1996): 701–26. For empirical support of this argument, see Helmut Anheier and Lester Salamon, *The Nonprofit Sector in the Developing World* (Manchester, England: Manchester University Press, 1998).

7. For more on religious motivations for work and volunteering, see Helen Rose Ebaugh, Paula F. Pipes, Janet Saltzman Chafetz, and Martha Daniels, "Where's the Religion? Distinguishing Faith-Based from Secular Social Service Agencies," *Journal for the Scientific Study of Religion* 42, no. 3 (2003): 411–26; John Bruce Nichols, *The Uneasy Alliance: Religion, Refugee Work, and U.S. Foreign Policy* (New York: Oxford University Press, 1988); and Robert Wuthnow and Virginia A. Hodgkinson, *Faith and Philanthropy in America: Exploring the Role of Religion in America's Voluntary Sector* (San Francisco: Jossey-Bass, 1990).

8. For more information on the practice of *zakat* and its role in aid in the Muslim world, see Jonathan Benthall and Jerome Bellion-Jourdan, *The Charitable Crescent: Politics of Aid in the Muslim World* (New York: St. Martin's Press, 2003). For more on the history and religious beliefs of the Druze, see Anis Obeid, *The Druze and Their Faith in Tawhid* (Syracuse, NY: Syracuse University Press, 2006).

9. For more on the distinctive characteristics of faith-based service providers, see Tamsin Bradley, "Does Compassion Bring Results? A Critical Perspective on Faith and Development" *Culture and Religion* 6, no. 3 (2005): 337–51; Mark Chaves and William Tsitsos, "Congregations and Social Services: What They Do, How They Do It, and with Whom," *Nonprofit & Voluntary Sector Quarterly* 30, no. 4 (2001): 660–83; and Ebaugh, Pipes, Saltzman Chafetz, and Daniels, 2003. For more on the effectiveness of FBOs, see Robert Fischer, "In God We Trust, All Others Bring Data: Assessing the State of Outcomes Measurement for Faith-Based and Community-Based Programming," in *Innovations in Effective Compassion: Compendium of Research Papers Presented at the Faith-Based and Community Initiatives Conference on Research, Outcomes, and Evaluation* (Washington, DC: US Department of Health and Human Services, 2008): 179–211. For more on the relationship among religiosity, positive behaviors, and health outcomes, see Byron R. Johnson, Ralph Brett Tompkins, and Derek Webb, *Objective Hope— Assessing the Effectiveness of Faith-Based Organizations: A Review of the Literature* (Philadelphia: University of Pennsylvania, Center for Research on Religion and Urban Civil Society, 2002).

10. For an assessment of the current state of evidence-based research on the effectiveness of faith-based service provision, see Fischer, 2008. For more on professionalism, philanthropic amateurism, and the social construction of FBO service recipients, see Lester Salamon, *Partners in Public Service: Government-Nonprofit Relations in the Modern Welfare State* (Baltimore, MD: Johns Hopkins University Press, 1995); and Bradley, 2005.

11. For more on the benefits of partnering with FBOs in development efforts, see Stephen V. Monsma, *When Sacred and Secular Mix:*

Religious Nonprofit Organizations and Public Money (Lanham, MD: Rowman and Littlefield, 1996); Nichols, 1988; and Wendy R. Tyndale, *Visions of Development: Faith Based Initiatives* (Aldershot, England: Ashgate Publishing Limited, 2006).

12. For more on the concept of compassion in Christian theology and its role in international development, see Bradley, 2005. For more on the concept of compassion in Buddhist teachings and its role in development, see Christopher Candland, "Faith as Social Capital: Religion and Community Development in Southern Asia," *Policy Sciences* 33 (2000): 355–74.

13. Bradley, 2005.

14. For more on Christian theology and development, see Erica Borstein, "Developing Faith: Theologies of Economic Development in Zimbabwe," *Journal of Religion in Africa* 32, no. 1 (2002): 4–31; Kirsteen Kim, *Concepts of Development in the Christian Traditions: A Religions and Development Background Paper, Working Paper No. 16* (Birmingham, England: Religions and Development Research Programme, University of Birmingham, 2007); and Sarah White and Romy Tiongco, *Doing Theology and Development: Meeting the Challenge of Poverty* (Edinburgh: Saint Andrew Press, 1997).

15. Anheier and Salamon, 1998; Rose-Ackerman, 1996.

16. Abul-Husn, 1998.

17. For more on the Armenian genocide and Armenians in Lebanon, see Robert Fisk, *The Great War for Civilisation: The Conquest of the Middle East* (New York: Alfred. A. Knopf, 2006). For more on Armenians as a social group in Lebanon, see Abul-Husn, 1998; and Johnson, 2002.

18. Abul-Husn, 1998.

19. Abul-Husn, 1998; Johnson, 2002.

20. For more on the Sabra and Shatila massacre, see Bayan Nuwayhed al-Hout, *Sabra and Shatila: September 1982* (Ann Arbor, MI: Pluto Press, 2004); Abba Eban, *The Beirut Massacre: The Complete Kahan Commission Report* (New York: Karz-Cohl, 1983); and Fisk, 2006.

21. For more on the nonprofit sector in the developing world, see Anheier and Salamon, 1998; and John Clark, *Democratizing Development: The Role of Voluntary Organizations* (West Hartford, CT: Kumarian Press, 1991). For more on power in social service environments, see Yeheskel Hasenfeld, "Power in Social Work Practice," *Social Service Review* 61, no. 3 (1987): 469–83.

3

Problems in Paradise

Violence, Fear, and Coercion in Sri Lanka's NGO Sector

Sri Lanka is a tropical green island in the Indian Ocean, sometimes romantically depicted as a teardrop dangling from the chin of India. Approximately the size of the US state of West Virginia, Sri Lanka is home to an ethnically, religiously, and linguistically diverse population of more than 20 million people. Much as in Lebanon, Sri Lanka's diversity has been a source of conflict, exclusion, and violence. The Liberation Tigers of Tamil Eelam (LTTE), or Tamil Tigers, often called the most innovative terrorist organization in the world, were born from many years of discrimination by the ethnic Sinhalese majority against Sri Lanka's ethnic Tamil minority. In the early 1980s the LTTE launched their military offensive aimed at establishing an independent homeland for Sri Lanka's Tamil minority, beginning one of the most prolonged and deadly ethnic conflicts in modern history. Since its beginning, Sri Lanka's civil war has killed close to 70,000 people, caused billions of dollars in damage, and displaced more than half a million people.[1]

However, much as in Lebanon, Sri Lanka's diversity not only has served as a source of conflict but also has generated a vibrant voluntary sector. Sri Lanka's civil society sector is strongly rooted in the island's various religious traditions, and it has existed since long before colonial times. A growing number of foreign international NGOs are present in the country as well, and currently a diverse array of indigenous and

PROPERTY OF
METHODIST UNIVERSITY LIBRARY

foreign faith-based and secular NGOs provide health and social services across the island.[2]

Violence in Sri Lanka and the Salience of Religion

Sri Lanka's population is composed of three primary ethnic groups: the Sinhalese (73.8 percent of the population), Sri Lankan Moors (7.2 percent of the population), and Indian and Sri Lankan Tamils (8.3 percent of the population). Another 10.3 percent of the population belong to other ethnic groups or are unspecified. Sri Lanka's civil war began in the early 1980s, when the LTTE initiated their military offensive against the Sri Lankan government in a struggle to create an independent homeland for the Tamil minority in the north and east of the island. The Tamils' grievance against the Sri Lankan government is based on decades of discrimination and exclusion following the country's independence from British colonial rule in 1948. The Sinhalese majority in Sri Lanka often portrays the Tamil minority as a newly arrived and unwelcome presence, but the Tamils of Sri Lanka are thought to have arrived on the island from south India during prehistoric times, although an additional Tamil community was brought to the island from India by British colonizers to work on tea plantations near the beginning of the twentieth century.[3]

Once the British granted Sri Lanka its independence, the Sinhala majority seized political power, refusing all power sharing with the Tamils. Because the Tamils were perceived as having received preferential treatment under British colonial rule, the Sinhala revoked many of the Tamils' basic civil rights in retribution; for example, Tamils were barred from holding positions in the army, bureaucracy, administration, and judiciary. The Official Language Act of 1956, which established Sinhala as the state's official language and effectively excluded the Tamil minority from many state institutions, was particularly damaging to ethnic relations. Consecutive Sri Lankan governments have carried out decades of segregation policies under the assumption that military dominance is the most effective way to control the minority Tamils. These policies have spawned a violent separatist movement, predominantly led by the LTTE, that has resulted in the deaths of tens of thousands of civilians. In February 2002 the LTTE and the government signed a cease-fire agreement that gave the LTTE control over Sri Lanka's northern and eastern provinces. However, violence and revenge attacks increased in 2006, with the LTTE and the Sri Lankan government both claiming they were only engaging in self-defense against the other party. In time the civil war resumed in full force, ending when the Sri Lankan state assumed control of LTTE-held territories in May 2009.[4]

As discussed in Chapter 1, the process of separating religious and ethnic identity is difficult, and in some cases impossible. On the surface this seems to be less of a challenge in Sri Lanka, because the conflict is almost always portrayed as an ethnic conflict between the Sinhalese majority and the Tamil minority. However, religion and ethnicity are more intertwined in Sri Lanka than is immediately apparent. Sri Lanka's civil war normally is not characterized as a religious conflict, given that the conflict is rooted in linguistic, ethnic, and political differences. However, the fact that the ethno-linguistic groups involved also are divided along religious lines adds an unavoidable religious dimension to the conflict. The Buddhist majority on the island (69.1 percent of the population) is primarily Sinhalese, whereas the Hindu community (7.1 percent of the population) is almost exclusively ethnically Tamil. Sri Lanka's sizable Christian and Muslim minorities (6.2 percent and 7.6 percent of the population, respectively) come from both the Sinhalese and the Tamil ethnic groups, although Muslims are sometimes characterized as their own separate ethnicity, Sri Lankan Moors. Buddhists, Hindus, Muslims, and Christians all have been affected by the ongoing civil war.

Since independence, politicians routinely have exploited religious differences among Sri Lanka's ethnic groups. This is most apparent in the Sinhalese Buddhist nationalist movements that periodically resurface in the country. Even though Tamil identity does not have an explicitly religious character, Sinhalese nationalist leaders have consistently emphasized the role of the Sinhalese as the divine protectors of Buddhism, supposedly chosen by Gautama Buddha to establish a Sinhalese-Buddhist society in Sri Lanka. This interpretation implies that the Tamil Hindu "unbelievers" represent a threat, and politicians warn that the Sinhalese should strive to prevent Tamils and Muslims from dominating the economy of the island. Citizens are free to practice any religion, but Sri Lanka's constitution grants Buddhism a "foremost position" in society and reaffirms Sinhala as the only official language of the island. In response, the LTTE has periodically targeted Buddhist religious sites during the civil war, most notably killing thirteen worshipers, including several children, in the 1998 bombing of the Temple of the Tooth, the holiest Buddhist shrine in the country.[5]

Meanwhile, Sri Lanka's Muslims have been the target of animosity from both the Sinhalese Buddhists and the Tamil community. The Buddhist Sinhalese have regarded the Muslims as "non-nationals" since the beginning of the twentieth century, and in 1990 the LTTE's leadership forcibly evicted virtually the entire Muslim population from the Northern Province as part of its ethnic cleansing program. Estimates of the number of people expelled vary from 46,000 to 75,000. Individuals were given up to twenty-four hours to leave the province, and tight restrictions on the types of property individuals were allowed to take meant that those expelled were left impoverished. More than fifteen years later, most of these individuals remain displaced and live in or near refugee centers, fearful of returning to their homes because of threats from the LTTE. However, even in this clear case of targeting a population based on religious identity, the lines between religion and ethnicity are unclear. The United States Department of State asserts that the LTTE's actions against Muslims are not due to Muslims' religious beliefs, but rather are part of an effort to rid the north and east of anyone who may be unsympathetic to their cause. As one scholar interviewed in Sri Lanka notes, "It is true that in Sri Lanka we refer to the Muslims by their religious identity. But when the Muslims were expelled from the north it was not about them being non-Hindu. Even though they speak Tamil, it was about them being a different community. So rather than religious, this was more of an ethnic cleansing."[6]

As was discussed in Chapter 1, theories of collective violence assert that in a context of violence, identity salience should be high, boundaries between groups should be activated, and individuals should differentiate between interactions within and among groups. In Sri Lanka we would expect religious identity to be salient in many communities. Ethnic identity is probably much more salient, but because ethnic groups are usually associated with a particular religion, religion becomes a salient identity category as well. The process of boundary activation between religious groups can create the potential for exclusionary and socially damaging behavior by NGO staff. As will be discussed later in the chapter, in Sri Lanka religious polarization is very evident in political rhetoric about NGOs and FBOs.

Religion and the Development of Sri Lanka's NGO Sector

The intertwined nature of ethnicity and religion in Sri Lanka means that even though ethnicity may be the most salient marker of identity in society, people are well aware of the religious identities associated with different communities. Religious identity has played a particularly important role in the development of Sri Lanka's local NGO sector. In Sri Lanka grassroots organizations spontaneously emerged in response to society's needs, and they have been part of Sri Lankan culture since ancient times. This system of grassroots organizations was somewhat weakened during the British colonial period, and the development of the local NGO sector became increasingly limited to organizations associated with religious institutions. Some of these organizations included committees associated with congregational service provision, such as temple societies in Hindu and Buddhist villages and mosque committees in Muslim villages, which engage in social welfare activities. However, as Christian missionaries became more involved in welfare and social development activities, a number of more formal church-based NGOs emerged. These Christian FBOs were soon mirrored by a number of Buddhist, Hindu, and Muslim organizations. Because these organizations were based in religious institutions, they evolved to be religiously and ethnically homogenous. After independence these FBOs received a certain amount of state support, which by the 1990s had led to the formation of separate government ministries for Buddhist, Hindu, and Islamic affairs. In contrast, Christian FBOs focused on establishing relationships with international donors. Although more inclusive organizations began to emerge over time, in Sri Lanka the notion that NGOs are affiliated with specific religious or ethnic groups has become strongly integrated into the public consciousness.[7]

Sri Lanka's NGO Sector: Violence, Animosity, and Conversion

As was noted in the previous chapter, the context of Lebanon's civil war played an important role in shaping the development of Lebanon's NGO sector. The same can be said of Sri Lanka's NGO sector. Although Sri Lanka has had a vibrant voluntary sector since before independence, currently many of Sri Lanka's NGOs are engaged in dealing with the negative effects of the civil war. Indeed, a number of local NGOs were created in response to the social needs produced by the conflict and the government's inability to provide basic services. Thus much of Sri Lanka's NGO sector has emerged as a response to violent conflict, and the sector's activities have been largely shaped by the needs created by the war.[8]

In addition to addressing needs created by the civil war, both local and international NGOs have been heavily involved in coping with the aftermath of the 2004 Asian tsunami. The tsunami killed nearly 40,000 Sri Lankans and led to a nearly immediate rise in the number of NGOs operating in Sri Lanka. According to the country's Central Bank, in the first five months following the tsunami, between 80 and 90 percent of all foreign aid was channeled through NGOs. Because of the corruption of previous Sri Lankan governments, most international donors felt they had little choice but to avoid using government ministries when distributing aid; they therefore chose to direct aid through NGOs. As will be discussed, this concentration of resources in the hands of the NGO community is one source of tension and anti-NGO sentiment among Sri Lanka's political leaders.[9]

Anti-NGO Sentiment in Sri Lanka

In contrast to Lebanon, where NGOs' war relief efforts and subsequent service provision have been well received by the public and the state, in Sri Lanka there is strong anti-NGO sentiment both in the political sphere and in the realm of public opinion. Politicians and the Sri Lankan public often view NGOs as corrupt entities that serve foreign interests and are in need of greater government control. This is not a new phenomenon. Since the 1950s both donor assistance and externally financed NGOs have met with suspicion, and suspicion continues to pervade political and bureaucratic attitudes in Sri Lanka toward NGOs, their activities, and their supporting donor agencies. However, numerous NGO employees in Sri Lanka report that recently, the hostility civil society actors feel from the Sri Lankan government and elements of Sinhalese civil society has reached new heights. Because of NGOs' involvement in issues of democratization, human rights, and assisting victims of the Tamil separatist conflict, in the early 1990s the Sri Lankan government began to view NGOs as overtly political and, as such, as a potential threat to the state. In a country previously subject to British, Dutch, and Portuguese colonial rule, many resent international donors and the NGO sector as a form of Western neo-colonialism. Anti-NGO sentiment in Sri Lanka seems to be fueled primarily by stories of NGO mismanagement and corruption and by the belief that the NGO community unfairly favors the Tamils and the LTTE in the civil war. A third and perhaps more inflammatory source of anti-NGO sentiment is fear of religious conversion by FBOs, which will be discussed later in the chapter.[10]

Stories of corruption and mismanagement in the NGO sector have played an important role in fueling anti-NGO sentiment in Sri Lanka. In the early 1990s, a government suspicious of the NGO community created an NGO Commission to investigate NGO affairs. The purpose of this commission was to investigate the NGO sector as a whole, but the only organizations that were investigated in any depth were a handful of NGOs that had been critical of government leadership. The commission reported that the NGO sector was almost entirely unregulated, with incidents of NGO workers unethically using their position and office to obtain money, property, and other benefits, including extravagant salaries and fringe benefits. Excerpts of the report were leaked to the media prior to its publication, thus increasing anti-NGO sentiment in the 1990s. The chaotic situation following the 2004 tsunami did not improve the image of the NGO community. In spite of the fact that the work performed by most NGOs indisputably prevented starvation and disease epidemics in the wake of the tsunami, the NGOs' failure to coordinate their efforts with one another and the resulting duplication of aid and waste of resources were viewed in a negative light. The Sri Lankan media highlighted the mistakes of the NGO community and gave considerably less attention to the positive benefits of NGO assistance.[11]

The perception that the NGO community is overly sympathetic to the Tamil minority is another factor feeding political and popular resentment of NGOs in government-controlled areas of Sri Lanka. Because much of the war-related destruction has occurred along the front lines between the Sri Lankan government's and the LTTE's territory, many NGOs operate in these predominantly Tamil areas. Thus they often are viewed as overly pro-Tamil, and some have even been charged with being active collaborators with the LTTE terrorist organization. Local NGOs that advocate peace and dialogue are often labeled unpatriotic by Sri Lanka's nationalist political parties and are accused of undermining the country's "war on terror." The perception that the NGO community favors the Tamil minority was not improved by the fact that nearly 60 percent of the death and destruction related to the tsunami took place along the northeast coast in provinces controlled by the LTTE, leading to even more NGO activity and funding being directed to these regions.[12] As Peter, an NGO staff member, put it, "There is resentment toward the NGOs. There is a general conception that NGOs work too much in LTTE areas, but this is where tsunami needs were the greatest. The government neglected these areas post-tsunami because politically they don't want to be seen as spending too much money in the Tamil heartland, so the NGOs had to move in. The truth is very few NGOs work directly with the LTTE—to do so would be suicide."

These concerns about NGOs being overly sympathetic to the LTTE at times lead to attention from the authorities. Roshini, an NGO staff member, described an incident that occurred at her NGO.

> We help whoever comes, we do not ask who they are or what their faith is or what their race is. Sometimes this causes problems, actually. Like some time ago, here in [my town, far outside LTTE areas], they thought I was working with the LTTE so my staff was arrested, and I was taken and questioned—that was because we work in the east. They thought that just because we help people in the east, then it has to be like that, we must be with the LTTE. But now people know, now generally they know that I work in the Tamil areas and the Sinhalese areas and I have no bias either way.

Sri Lanka's anti-NGO sentiment has taken a violent, and at times deadly, turn. By far the most notable act of violence against the NGO community was the execution of seventeen ethnic Tamil aid workers from the French NGO Action Against Hunger in August 2006. Fifteen aid workers were found shot in the head in the agency's office, and another two appeared to have been shot while fleeing the scene. This event was the deadliest attack on humanitarian workers worldwide since the bombing of the United Nations offices in Baghdad in August 2003, where twenty-two people were killed. Major General Ulf Henricsson, the head of the mission charged with monitoring the ceasefire between the Sri Lankan government and the LTTE, assigned blame for the massacre to the Sri Lankan government's security forces. This incident was extreme, but NGO workers in Sri Lanka's north and east are frequently the target of grenade attacks, attacks by angry mobs, and harassment and threats. In fact, the majority of staff members from Sri Lankan NGOs indicated that their NGO had been the target of violent actions or threats at some point during their operation. A number of staff members attributed at least some of the attacks on their organizations to the Sri Lankan government. Deepal describes an attack on his NGO that he thinks may have been a warning to leave the front lines between government and LTTE territory, where the fighting is most fierce. "Last week these seventeen aid workers were executed, and that was quite probably the government who executed them. But that wasn't the first incident; there has been a campaign to get the NGOs out. We got a hand grenade in our office on a Sunday, and two other NGOs as well. The office was empty but it was a very clear warning. 'Now get out, get lost.' Maybe this was sort of a pre-warning, 'Get out because it's going to get hairy here, and don't be here because you're going to put yourself at risk.' It's quite possible. I'm still not sure."

Another reason why the Sri Lankan government may be targeting NGOs, mentioned by several staff members as well as international observers, is that they would prefer not to have witnesses to their combat with the LTTE. Robert explains, "The government does not want international witnesses to the fighting and how it is being conducted. They want to fight the war without prying eyes. Neither side respects normal combat rules and, the truth is, expats have more clout with the international community. So it is best if you can just prevent the expats from seeing anything."

In addition to physical attacks on NGOs, nearly all staff members mentioned bureaucratic hurdles that have been imposed to limit NGOs' access to the northern and eastern provinces of the country. Foreign staff members in particular have been the target of these regulations. Oftentimes when on the border with LTTE-controlled areas, foreign nationals are informed that they need a special entry permit from officials in the capital. Once they arrive at the appropriate ministry in Colombo, they are told that no such permit exists. The government reportedly also is refusing foreign residency permits and work permits in greater numbers, mainly targeting employees of NGOs. In addition to normal struggles to bring supplies into the north and east, these hurdles have made it increasingly difficult for NGO staff to conduct their work. Whether these efforts will succeed at pushing out foreign NGOs remains to be seen. Many of the foreign NGO staff members seemed intent on remaining in the country as long as possible. As Clare notes, "I think the very, very worrying thing around the world is the way humanitarian relief is being politicized by different governments for their own purposes. And of course here the government doesn't want humanitarian agencies in the north and the east because they don't want witnesses to what happens. And if they want to get rid of witnesses, the way to do that is to vilify NGOs and to force them out. But then we have to say that we won't go, we have to stay and be a witness."

FBOs and Sri Lanka's Anti-Conversion Movement

This description of Sri Lanka's high degree of anti-NGO sentiment helps one better understand the potency of resentment against religious organizations. Although employees of FBOs around the world are interested in serving the material needs of the poor, they are interested in meeting service recipients' spiritual needs as well, and this interest has caused a great deal of apprehension in Sri Lanka. Research on faith-based nonprofit service provision in the United States and the developing world shows that many nonprofit organizations are involved in evangelistic and missionary work in conjunction with service delivery. As discussed in the case of Lebanon, staff members often focus on both material and spiritual needs and may explicitly integrate religious practice into their service provision. Research shows that whereas many service recipients are aware of the role faith plays in nonprofit organizations, they may appreciate it in differing degrees. Some service recipients value the religious orientation of staff members and even report that faith-based social service programs provide them with a ministry opportunity and a chance to serve others while serving themselves. In the United States, service recipients who share a sense of religious solidarity with service providers, particularly in African American Christian communities, sometimes report feeling more comfortable in religious social service settings. However, in some settings service recipients report resenting sermons and being resistant to religious practice, even in cases where service recipients share the same religious background as the staff of the FBO serving them.[13]

In Sri Lanka there is a strong fear that FBOs, in particular international FBOs, have come to the island with the intention of converting Sri Lankans of all religious groups to an evangelic Protestant form of Christianity. This fear is an additional source of strong anti-NGO sentiment in the country, and it has sparked several movements to pass anti-conversion legislation in the Parliament. In addition to fueling anti-NGO sentiment, concerns about forced religious conversion have led to an increase in the number of attacks on Christian churches in the country, particularly by Buddhist extremist groups. But even though Buddhist politicians have been the most vocal about forced conversion, Sri Lanka's Catholic community has also expressed concern about more recently arrived evangelic groups.[14]

Reports of forced conversion and "allurement" to Christianity by missionaries and FBOs have led to several anti-conversion bills being presented to Sri Lanka's Parliament. During the early 2000s, the Buddhist nationalist party Jathika Hela Urumaya (JHU) and Sri Lanka's Minister of Buddhist Affairs presented a variety of anti-conversion bills to the Parliament and the Cabinet, although so far, these bills have been held unconstitutional. The bills typically criminalize conversion, requiring new converts to register with the government when they change their religion and imposing fines or imprisonment on persons convicted of "unethically" converting another person to their religion. Stiffer penalties are typically included for conversion of vulnerable groups such as children, prisoners, people with disabilities, and refugees.[15]

In addition to concerns about proselytization by churches and missionaries, Christian fundamentalists in Sri Lanka have been accused of using humanitarian NGOs as a facade for their evangelic activities. Some groups contend that Christians engage in aggressive evangelism and take advantage of societal problems such as general poverty, war, and lack of education. This contention was buoyed by the highly publicized work of a subset of evangelic Christian FBOs that used tsunami aid to spread their religious message. At times the Sri Lankan government has been criticized by senior religious leaders for not making the problem of conversion its top policy priority. Government officials have suggested that efforts at conversion threaten to disrupt the existing religious harmony in Sri Lanka and that they define religious conversion as a security issue.[16]

In this context, the humanitarian activities of FBOs have been specifically targeted by anti-conversion legislation as a form of "allurement." One proposed bill defines allurement as "any temptation in the form of: (1) any gift or gratification whether in cash or kind; (2) grant of any material benefit, whether monetary or otherwise; (3) grant of employment or grant of promotion in employment."[17] It is easy to see that many of the humanitarian activities of FBOs might fall within this definition.

Christians counter that their humanitarian work is sincere and is not focused on conversion. Sri Lanka's Catholic Bishops' Conference and the National Christian Council remind political leaders that all religions compel their followers to do charitable works and that it would be wrong to label all such acts as efforts at conversion. In 2004 United Nations Special Rapporteur on Freedom of Religion Asma Jahangir concluded that accusations of forced or coerced conversion were vague and no direct testimonies were available. However, she admitted that second-hand reports by reliable sources show that conversions through inappropriate means have sometimes taken place. In interviews conducted for this book, some FBO staff indicated that evangelism indeed was a specific goal of their humanitarian work, as will be described later in the chapter.[18]

The environment in which NGOs in Sri Lanka operate is described in detail in an effort to better place in context the interviews with NGO staff that will be presented later in the chapter. At the time when these interviews were conducted, both faith-based and secular NGOs in Sri Lanka operated in circumstances shaped by the natural disaster of the tsunami and the humanitarian disaster of war. NGOs were frequently the targets of violent attacks on their staff and their facilities, and they were also the subject of a great deal of public and political controversy, resentment, and suspicion. Faith-based NGOs in particular were vilified by the media and by political leaders. This context is significantly different from that of Lebanon or, as will be discussed in Chapter 4, that of Bosnia and Herzegovina.

The Role of Faith in Sri Lankan Social Service NGOs

Much as in Lebanon, in Sri Lanka faith often played an important role in the motivations of staff members from Buddhist, Christian, and Muslim

73

FBOs.[19] However, two interesting patterns arose that did not appear in the FBO community in Lebanon. First, slightly less than half of the staff members from Christian FBOs and all staff members from Muslim FBOs mentioned that although their organization had faith origins, it now operated as a secular organization. Interestingly, all Christian FBO staff members who mentioned this process of secularization were from international foreign NGOs operating in Sri Lanka. This reflects a historical trend of secularization among older Catholic and mainline Protestant international FBOs that has been matched by an upswing in the number of evangelic Christian FBOs becoming engaged in international relief and development.[20] As Hans, an employee of an international Christian FBO explained, "We are not faith-based in the traditional US sense, but in a Northern European sense. We consider it a question of morals and ethics rather than faith, which is based in Christian teachings of course, but long ago. Actually, our organization's constitution specifically states that evangelism is prohibited. We are not about promoting faith, but about promoting care for humanity and basic rights. Because of this difference [our NGO] sometimes clashes with other faith-based NGOs who have more direct goals of evangelism."

It is important to note that not all international Christian FBOs included in the study mentioned this process of secularization. A number of staff members from international Christian FBOs felt that faith played a very important role in their organization's work.

A second interesting trend that appeared in Sri Lanka but not in Lebanon or Bosnia and Herzegovina is that the staff of several NGOs, while not affiliated with any specific faith tradition, expressed that they would be uncomfortable if their organization were to be categorized as secular. Staff of these nondenominational faith-based NGOs instead insisted that they should be thought of as "spiritual" and expressed a strong commitment to the value that faith brings to people's lives, regardless of the particular faith they profess. As Palitha, a staff member from a "spiritual" NGO, put it, "Our organization is not religious, no. But it is spiritual, and spirituality is for everybody. Spirituality is at the core and everybody needs it. If a Buddhist comes to me I will speak to him based on his own philosophy. If a Hindu comes to me, I will speak to him based on his philosophy. There is a powerful spiritual component here. I cannot speak about the work of other organizations. But in my case, I know that spirituality takes us forward."

As we will see in Chapter 4, the secularization of faith-based NGOs is a trend that also appeared in Bosnia and Herzegovina, but the spiritual orientation of NGOs with no historical ties to any religious tradition was a pattern unique to Sri Lanka.

Profession, Personal Ties, and Faith in Service Provision

Just as in Lebanon, in Sri Lanka religious identity and religious beliefs influence NGO staff members' choices about their careers in the nonprofit sector. More than 80 percent of all staff members indicated that their professional training and/or past professional experience in health and social services was one factor that led them to work for their NGO. However, personal ties within particular religious communities, as well as religious belief and inspiration also played an important role in leading many staff members to work for their organization, although personal ties seem to play less of a role in Sri Lanka than they do in Lebanon. Just over one-third of all the staff members mentioned that their personal ties within a particular religious community had led them to work for their NGO. Much as in Lebanon, these personal ties typically involved a member of a religious congregation informing them of the availability of the job and referring them to the individual responsible for hiring, or their own personal ties to the NGO via previous volunteer work through a religious congregation. Friendships with members of a religious group and personal relationships with charismatic religious leaders also played a role. Staff members from "spiritual" FBOs and half of the staff members from Buddhist FBOs indicated that they had come to work for their organization through personal ties they had within the religious community. Just less than half of staff members from Christian FBOs indicated that they had come to work for their organization through personal ties they had within the religious community, and interestingly, none of these were from international Christian FBOs that had report-edly become secular over time. This may indicate that personal ties play an important role for local Christian FBOs but a less important role for secularized international Christian FBOs. In contrast, no participants from Muslim FBOs mentioned that they had come to their job through per-sonal ties within their religious community.

In striking contrast to Lebanon, one very interesting aspect of the role that personal connections play in Sri Lanka is that, although many NGO workers came to work for their NGO via their personal ties to a religious community, these ties were not necessarily within *their own* re-ligious community. As John, a staff member from a Christian FBO noted, "We all came to work here because we are all friends of the church. But in the office not everyone is [our Christian denomination], and not every-one is Christian. We are all friends of the church, but we have a mixture of Christian denominations and also other religions. Also, we are a mix-ture of Tamils and Sinhalese."

Manoj, a staff member from a Buddhist FBO, explained how he came to his position. "When I was a university student I met [the founder of the NGO]. I am Tamil, and I am not Buddhist. But he asked me if I would like to work for him and I said yes. When I saw the good work [the NGO] was doing, I couldn't say no. If you met [the founder of the NGO] and sat and talked with him, maybe by the end you would find yourself working here too."

In addition to mentioning personal ties, just as in Lebanon, a num-ber of staff explained their career choice as being motivated by their religious belief and religious inspiration. Staff members from Buddhist FBOs were most likely to indicate that religious belief or religious in-spiration was one of the factors that drew the individual to work for the organization. Staff members from "spiritual" and Christian FBOs also in-dicated that religious belief or religious inspiration was one of the factors that drew them to their work. Once again, there is a difference between secular international Christian FBOs and other Christian FBOs; no staff members from secularized FBOs reported that religious belief or reli-gious inspiration had drawn them to work for their organization. In ad-dition, no participants from Muslim FBOs mentioned being drawn to their work by religious belief or inspiration, which stands in stark contrast to staff members from Muslim FBOs in Lebanon and in Bosnia and Herzegovina, as will be discussed in Chapter 4. This may be because many staff members of Muslim FBOs reported serving Muslims because they are an oppressed ethnic community within Sri Lanka, rather than because they share a sense of religious solidarity with their service recipients.

The sense that faith demands social action was strong for many staff members from both Buddhist and Christian FBOs. As Samanmali from a Buddhist FBO explained,

"In Buddhism we believe that if we have trust for someone, they are our relative. If I can trust you, you are my sister, even if you are not Buddhist. If my own brother betrays me, then can I say he is my relative? If your father or brother would betray you, they are not your relative. So all people who we can trust are our relatives, and we must help them."

Whereas staff from Buddhist FBOs tended to cite similar "familial" or communal obligations to offer assistance, staff from Christian FBOs, much as in Lebanon, tended to refer to the formal teachings of Christianity and Biblical scripture:

> You could say in a sense that the work that we do is a witness to our faith. It's a commandment that you should love your neighbor, but there's nothing in there about it being your Christian neighbor. And you know, "whoever does it to the least of my brethren does it to me"; there's lots of things. I mean personally, if I am doing talks for [some NGOs], I would talk about Matthew 25, about the sheep and the goats, and clothing people, looking after the homeless, the prisoners, things like that. So, in essence, the work on the ground might not look any different, but the motivation for doing it might be different, in the sense that we do it because we believe that our faith demands it of us.

The Added Benefits of Faith

Echoing staff members in Lebanon and reflecting research on FBOs in the United States and the developing world, a number of staff members in Sri Lanka felt that religious identity gives some form of added value to the services they render.[21] Just less than half of the staff members interviewed felt that the faith orientation of their NGO increased the quality of the services they provided. The staff members who indicated there was an added value to their services included all staff from "spiritual" and Buddhist FBOs and just over half of staff members from Christian FBOs. Once again a similar pattern appears, in that those participants from secularized international Christian FBOs did not mention that faith brought added value to their organization. No staff members from Muslim FBOs indicated that faith added value to the services they provided, again standing in contrast to staff from Muslim FBOs in Lebanon and Bosnia and Herzegovina. The added benefits that staff members perceived faith as bringing to their organizations' work included

- less conflict and greater trust among NGO staff
- greater respect and cultural sensitivity
- less corruption and more accountability
- more effective service provision thanks to church networks

Interestingly, these benefits differ substantially from those mentioned by staff of FBOs operating in Lebanon, and they also differ from those typically mentioned in the literature on FBOs in the United States. The FBO staff interviewed did not mention more individualized and compassionate service provision or more highly committed and motivated workers as benefits, but both of these are heavily emphasized as benefits in the literature on FBOs in the United States and were also mentioned by the staff of FBOs operating in Lebanon. In fact, the only benefit mentioned by staff members in both Lebanon and Sri Lanka was less conflict and greater trust among NGO staff.

Less Conflict and Greater Trust Among Staff
Much as in Lebanon, some staff members indicated that they believe the faith orientation of their organization results in less conflict and greater trust among workers in the organization. Whereas in Lebanon staff members from both Christian and Muslim FBOs mentioned this as

a benefit of their faith orientation, in Sri Lanka only participants from Christian FBOs mentioned this benefit. This seems to be due to a sense that staff members have a shared identity and a shared vision for the work of the organization, which results in less internal conflict. Irene, a staff member from a Christian FBO, noted that "Our staff members are explicitly Christian, and actually everyone has to write a story about their own faith commitment as part of the process of being hired. But we will accept people from any denomination, as long as they are Christian. Because we are Christians, we have a commitment to the vision of helping people, and that overarching commitment helps in dealing with internal power struggles. I think we have less problems because in the end we all agree on our faith."

Greater Respect and Cultural Sensitivity
For several staff members in Sri Lanka, another added benefit of being a faith-based organization was that their faith orientation gave them greater respect for their service recipients and made them more culturally sensitive. Participants from Buddhist, Christian, and "spiritual" NGOs all saw this as an important value that their faith added to their service delivery. David, a staff member from a Christian NGO, believes that

> missionaries are often more culturally sensitive and effective than other, maybe secular aid agencies. A lot of aid agencies have a very rigid agenda, like with gender and development, they have decided they should have a certain kind of gender development program and they come in already believing there are clear right and wrong ways of doing things. So they leave little room for compromise. But missionaries are trained to be culturally sensitive. Missionaries use Christian teaching to examine both the local culture and the culture of the aid worker in ways that are critical of and affirming of both cultures. Then we leave room for the Holy Spirit to come in and find a balance between the two, a balance that works for the people we are here to help.

Several staff members from Buddhist FBOs noted that, because Buddhism affirms all religions, they are more easily able to work with other religious communities, including geographic areas with very few Buddhists such as the Tamil areas on the north of the island.

> We respect and we accept all religions, all the teachings of the famous leaders who have been important to human beings. These teachings are common to all people. All the religious leaders have given good ideas to create a good society in the world, and we respect and follow all their concepts. First we go to the Buddhist temple and we talk to the monks and we get their advice, but if there are other religious leaders in the village then we also work with them to get their advice. If we organize some project in the village, we invite all the religious leaders to come. And in the north the Tamil and Muslim people live together, but there are not really any Sinhala people, there are not any Buddhist people there. But still, we work in the north with those people, and they accept us and love us.

Less Corruption and Greater Accountability

In a country where accusations of NGO corruption run rampant, several staff from both Buddhist and Christian FBOs indicated that they felt the faith orientation of the NGO caused their organizations to have lower levels of corruption and a greater degree of accountability. Claude, a staff member from a Christian FBO, describes his organization's greater accountability in this way: "Now, there has been corruption all over, and I cannot say that because we are a faith-based organization we don't ever have corruption, but I do think there is more general accountability. Things are raised much quicker. I know cases at other NGOs where things are ignored or swept under the carpet. But at [our NGO] if someone finds out something inappropriate is going on the issue is raised and it is dealt with right away."

More Effective Service Provision
Thanks to Church Networks

All of the staff members from Christian FBOs who mentioned that they believed that their religious identity added value to their organizations also mentioned some way in which church networks enabled them to be more effective service providers. For international NGOs, this often was due to the fact that churches gave them broader access to the community and provided them with partners who had intimate knowledge of their community's needs.

> We do have an extra network that [other NGOs] don't have, and that's the churches, and that does help. We have a very elaborate network throughout the country, national alliances, and contacts locally with churches, and our staff are members of churches, and that network helps. Sometimes when there are things we can't do, the churches can do them.

> Of course there's a huge advantage because you are working with clergy and people who know their communities, know who the people are, if a project proposal comes in, then a (local church partner) officer can go make a field visit and he can double check some things with them, that the beneficiaries are real beneficiaries.

Another benefit frequently mentioned was that, in a country mired by anti-NGO sentiment where bureaucratic barriers are often placed in the path of NGO work, churches could often accomplish tasks that NGOs simply could not. Lily told the following story: "In the east at the moment, where there is increasing resistance from the military to allowing the NGOs to work in certain areas, I talked to [a church partner] yesterday and they managed to get two trucks in through the south, and the reason they could do that is because it wasn't from an NGO. Because it was from a church, the military let it through. And the other day, [one reverend and his colleagues] went into Muttur, it was just after the massacre (of seventeen aid workers), and they were able to get in because they were with a church, they weren't an NGO. Again, this is the advantage of having local church partners."

Working through church partners was seen to be a particular advantage when operating in LTTE-controlled areas, because the LTTE often "taxes" NGOs and exercises tight control over the NGO sector in their territory. Scholars have noted that as a consequence of their ongoing efforts at war relief, the Catholic Church in particular has been able to gain the trust of the LTTE, to the extent that it has been able to raise concerns with LTTE leadership about sensitive issues such as recruitment of child soldiers.[22] Indrani describes how church networks assist her FBO when working in LTTE-controlled areas: "In the areas that we are working, we are working through the clergy, and through the churches. So the churches have been there for many many years before the tsunami, so they already have relationships with the LTTE. I certainly think there are difficulties working in these areas in terms of attempts by the LTTE for taxation. But again, the churches and things have a long relationship with the LTTE so some of those things are easier to deal with, and the people aren't new, so they have a long-term relationship."

Religion as a Service Rendered

The interviews in Sri Lanka presented an interesting pattern that was similar to one found in Lebanon. For a number of staff members from FBOs, religion not only was assumed to add value to the services provided by the organization but actually was portrayed as one of the services the organization renders. Whereas in Lebanon this was an exclusively Christian phenomenon, in Sri Lanka only one of the staff members who described religion as a service offered to clients was from a Christian FBO. Instead, the majority of staff members were from Buddhist FBOs, and other staff members worked with "spiritual" and Muslim FBOs. In fact, all staff members from Muslim FBOs mentioned religious activities as one of the services they provided. This finding among Muslim FBOs in Sri Lanka might seem particularly surprising, given that all staff members from Muslim FBOs mentioned the secularization of their organization. None of the staff members felt faith added value to their organizations' work, and religious ties and religious belief seem to play little role in how employees came to their positions. However, as will be discussed later, staff members from Muslim FBOs report that their organizations serve an almost exclusively Muslim population, and scheduled religious activities were offered based on the requests of their service recipients. Fatima, a staff member from a Muslim FBO, described this: "We also have religious activities for them, because it is majority Muslims, but we do adapt ourselves to suit the region, the ethnic groups, the religion and how it is practiced in that area. Faith is not a problem here. When it comes to the Islamic issues, we have a Muslim to teach about it, but our staff is multi-cultural. And anything we do, unless it is really religiously based, we try to involve other communities."

Staff members from Buddhist and Christian FBOs also discussed tangible scheduled activities that they conduct with service recipients. Whereas a staff member from a Christian FBO described Bible studies and prayer meetings, staff members from Buddhist FBOs most often discussed meditation. As Chaminda, a staff member from a Buddhist FBO, put it, "One important service we have is that we have a meditation center, it is a center for Buddhist teachings but open to all people. Meditation is a very important part of a holistic approach to community improvement. We teach meditation to pregnant mothers, prisoners, school children, the old people, even foreigners if they want. People from different religions even learn to meditate from us, because meditation is good for everyone, it is something everyone needs. It is important for control, peace, and discipline."

In addition to descriptions of concrete scheduled religious activities, there was also a strong sense among staff members that spiritual development is an essential component of any type of relief and development work, and that it was therefore an extremely important part of their activities. This sense seemed to be present among participants from Buddhist, Christian, and "spiritual" FBOs alike. As Romaine, a staff member from a Christian FBO asserted, "I think the religious mission is very important for the person. We can give them an education and a meal, but if that person doesn't know Christ, then I think that person will perish. That's what the Bible says. So it is good if we can share Christ with the person, and build him up, build up the spiritual side of the person. Being a holistic ministry, we are not just looking at his physical needs, we are looking at the spiritual also. This is part of the services we provide, and all our workers address the spiritual side, as well as the physical. All our staff are Christian, and all our staff do this, conduct Bible studies and prayer sessions."

Or as Chaya, a staff member from a Buddhist FBO, said, "At the same time we are trying to give them basic needs, we are not thinking only of economic development and social development. Development also includes spiritual development. Economic development, social development, and spiritual development all come together to make a good society in the village. We cannot only provide for basic needs or economic development. We want to make good people in the village. That is also part of development. That's why we also focus on spiritual development."

However, particularly among staff members from Buddhist FBOs and "spiritual" FBOs, there was an assertion that faith of any sort, regardless of the religion, was a positive force in people's lives and should be fostered by FBOs in their service provision. As Dilini, a staff member from a Buddhist FBO noted, "It is very important for the children that they should have a religion, so they can get a fear of God or a fear for religion. They should have some fear for something. If they fear not to go to heaven or they fear a bad incarnation or they fear something else, it is good. Then they can learn to be loyal, they can learn to work hard to be good, and they can feel they will be rewarded in some way. These values are very important, and we try to promote them."

Jagath, a staff member from a "spiritual" FBO, made a similar point: "Spirituality is for everybody. Spirituality is at the core and everybody needs it. Here, the Catholics pray morning, noon, and evening. And the Buddhists pray their own way, and we take them to the temple once a month. Those who can be taken to the church, they are taken once a week. The Buddhists pray separately, and those who like, they come and join the Catholics after their chanting for the Catholic service. A lot of people like to participate in both, and why not? Both give them good benefits."

These excerpts make it clear that the idea that service provision and development are holistic ventures that must encompass both physical conditions and the spirit is not unique to Christian philosophy, as was discussed in Chapter 2 on Lebanon. This sense of holistic development is also central to Buddhist philosophy in Sri Lanka. For example, the Sarvodaya Shramadana Movement, a network of Buddhist village-based development initiatives throughout the island, portrays development as a process of "awakening" that must address spiritual, moral, cultural, social, economic, and political development in order to truly be effective. This holistic vision of development seems to have been embraced by the nondenominational staff of self-described "spiritual" FBOs as well.[23]

Religious Divides and Service Provision

In many cultures, religious institutions are one of the first groups people turn to for help, which is part of the reason for the emergence of FBOs worldwide. This reliance on religious bodies for social help is also evident in Sri Lanka, and one Buddhist monk explained how it came into play following the 2004 tsunami. "After the tsunami, people came to temples, mosques, churches, and other religious places in order to feel that they were in a safe place; they felt that there was a certain spiritual protection that came from these houses of worship. But then they never left, because they had nowhere to go. Then these religious places became de facto refugee camps. Therefore the temples and other religious places had to start providing aid and relief."

As was discussed earlier, religion has played a strong role in shaping the evolution of Sri Lanka's NGO sector, beginning before colonial times. However, whereas NGO social service provision is clearly structured along religious lines in Lebanon, in Sri Lanka this does not seem to be the case. All staff members from Christian, "spiritual," and secular NGOs indicated that their NGO serves a religiously mixed group of participants, and more than 80 percent of staff members from Buddhist FBOs made the same assertion. Staff members from Buddhist FBOs who indicated that their FBOs served primarily Buddhists attributed this to the geographic location of the FBO and the primarily Buddhist population of the neighborhood.

However, all staff members from Muslim FBOs indicated that their FBOs served an almost exclusively Muslim population. One staff member who worked in women's empowerment programs indicated that a religiously mixed group of beneficiaries would not be tolerated by the men in the women's families and therefore would render the programs irrelevant. However, other workers from Muslim NGOs stated that Muslim women were specifically targeted for services because of their uniquely marginalized position in the community:

> Our main topic is Muslim women, not because of any bias or anything, but because they are the most marginalized. We have been researching on violence against women, and the Muslim community has a hierarchy of men, a domination, and violence is a big problem. Now, we are trying to have a breakthrough with an awareness program, teaching Muslim women their rights using the Koran. Because the Sharia law, if it is done as it is actually written in the Koran, then the women, they will get their rights. So we are trying to teach the right interpretation of the Koran, because by saying it in these religious terms, we can get the community to listen more.

Although social service provision in Sri Lanka does not seem to be divided along religious lines, some staff members from local Christian FBOs did mention that there was pressure in their parishes to serve Christians before serving other people, particularly following the tsunami. As Anjelo, a staff member from a local Christian FBO explained,

> In the very beginning we felt we knew there were parishioners who were affected, so we had a need to help them. Then after we helped them, after that we never asked if people were Christian or non-Christian. Christians are a very very small minority here, so we could finish helping them quickly. A lot of the affected people are either Hindus, Muslims, or Buddhists, so the vast majority of work has actually benefited Hindus, Muslims, and Buddhists. This has actually caused some problems with some parishioners who believe that charity begins at home, that kind of thing. But we wanted to make an effort to be blind to the whole religious issue, and to respond to need, and the need was really with the other religious groups.

Religious Tensions in the Field

In Sri Lanka, service provision seems not to be structured along religious lines except in the case of Muslim FBOs. In fact, much as in

Lebanon, many of the staff members gave examples of ways in which their religious teachings encourage inclusive service provision. However, in spite of the inclusive service provision reported by the staff members, religious tensions presented numerous challenges to staff members providing services on the ground. These included perceptions by the local community that service provision was based on religion or ethnicity, tensions between international donors and community requests to rebuild places of worship, and widespread concerns about FBO evangelism.

Perceptions of Discrimination

Even though FBO staff insisted their service provision was inclusive, in Sri Lanka the pervasive public perception is that faith-based organizations serve only people of the same faith.[24] Many staff members reported that it took a great deal of effort to prove to community members that they provided services regardless of faith or ethnicity. Numerous FBO staff indicated that their organization worked in cooperation with local religious leaders of other faiths and even formed multireligious committees to select service recipients in an effort to demonstrate the inclusive nature of their work. Over time, most FBO staff reported that their organizations had been able to establish a good reputation in the communities where they worked and were now involved in providing services to a diverse group of recipients. However, suspicions and accusations persist and still create problems for FBO staff. Sara told the following story: "[One of our partners], was pulled out of a truck and threatened with a gun, and he was questioned why [his NGO] didn't aid Muslims. And when he said, 'Well, actually, we do, we work in Afghanistan and Iraq and places,' then the guy said, 'Okay' and he took the gun away. That's worrying."

The question of how much aid is channeled to Sinhala, Tamil, and Muslim communities has become politically charged in nature. Muslim communities in particular feel that they have been discriminated against in aid provision. Muslims were disproportionately affected by the tsunami because of their concentration in the east of the island, yet many Muslims feel that tsunami aid has been channeled disproportionately toward Tamil communities.[25]

Reconstructing Houses of Worship

Another source of tension mentioned by several staff members from Christian FBOs was their inability to assist with the reconstruction of religious places of worship following the tsunami, in spite of requests from members of the community. This was often attributed to the fact that international religious donors would be displeased by reconstruction of non-Christian places of worship if they were made aware of such activities. Other staff members also mentioned that, as signatories to the International Red Cross/Red Crescent Code of Conduct, they are not allowed to engage in overtly religious activities such as constructing buildings for religious use. John describes how his Christian FBO attempts to address these requests. "One major problem for a resettlement project is that people will always want support to rebuild their temple, their Hindu temple, or their mosque, and it's something we just can't get into. We will run into problems at home if we do. Where we do help them, is in an area where there are Muslims and Hindus and Catholics, or different groups, we will organize a joint cleaning day and then people from all the groups help to clean out the mosque, and clean out the temple, and clean out the church. Then all of the rehabilitation work they do independently, and we don't fund them, we just organize them to work together."

In contrast, Buddhist FBOs seemed to have more freedom in this regard. Chanaka, a staff member from a Buddhist FBO explains that "They all have their own culture, in the Muslim community and the Sinhala community and the Tamil community. They have their own culture and we don't want to violate their culture. If we are going to live together we have to respect each other and they can believe their faith. If they want a Hindu temple in the village, then we will give them a temple, or also a mosque if they want, because we know the activities are different."

Concerns About FBO Evangelism

As noted earlier, fear of conversion—in particular, promotion of conversion to Protestant Christianity by Christian FBOs—has become an inflammatory political issue in Sri Lanka and is the subject of attention from reporters and legislators alike. Many staff members from Christian

FBOs felt threatened by this anti-conversion movement, and especially by anti-conversion legislation, because they felt it would restrict their freedom of expression and their freedom to assist the poor. In particular, several staff members believed that anti-conversion legislation, if passed, would allow officials to portray many types of humanitarian aid as efforts at "allurement" and therefore would give officials even more power to push NGOs out of the country. According to Tania, a staff member from a Christian FBO, "Under this bill, providing aid can be construed as conversion. But this bill is a violation of our fundamental rights. We should have the freedom to give help to others without being afraid. As I understand it, the only other countries that have this kind of legislation are places like Iran. We are supposed to be a democracy."

In Sri Lanka, as in many other countries, concern regarding conversion is related to the idea that people experiencing poverty and other related problems can be subtly coerced to change religions when FBOs offer financial and other incentives. These concerns are quite reasonable, given that scholars often discuss recruiting adherents as one possible goal of faith-based social service providers. As was discussed in Chapter 1, social service providers hold notable power over service recipients, particularly the poor and vulnerable. The power of an organization over a service recipient is directly proportional to the individual's need for the organization's services, and service providers have a considerable power advantage when individuals have few or no alternative service providers in their communities. This power advantage allows service providers, should they choose, to exercise substantial control over service recipients' lives. In a context like Sri Lanka, where many individuals have a dire need for services because of the effects of the 2004 tsunami and ongoing ethnic conflict, one can easily imagine how ethical concerns arise when individuals are dependent on services provided by an FBO interested in evangelism. In Sri Lanka there is an additional perception that although FBOs may offer aid to everyone, the quality and quantity of aid offered to those who formally join their church are higher.[26]

More than 90 percent of staff members from FBOs in Sri Lanka made no statements indicating that evangelism was a specific goal of their organization. However, several staff members indicated that they had been accused of conversion at various points during their organization's history. As Anders, a staff member from a Christian FBO, recounts,

> In Sri Lanka faith-based NGOs are very stigmatized, especially if they aren't Buddhist NGOs. This makes it difficult to work, especially in the south where there is more Buddhist nationalist sentiment. So lots of times [our NGO] works through local partners who are not faith-based in order to avoid these tensions. The faith-based NGOs are always criticized in media, and actually [our NGO] was accused of conversion by the newspapers just based on our name, even though at this point we are almost secular and we certainly don't have any religious activities. Finally we decided just to lay low rather than respond to the article in hopes it would blow over. NGOs as a whole are often the target of media scrutiny, but especially the faith-based NGOs.

Those staff members whose FBOs were not engaged in evangelism typically reported that over time, local communities would come to see that they were not engaged in conversion, and trust would begin to build. As Alex notes, "They [non-Christian NGOs and community leaders] were willing to work with us because they saw that we had no ulterior motives. They saw that we were not there to convert, which some churches do, but we have made a very strong effort never to do that. So we ended up being approached by people who had never approached us before, which is very good. And now we are working with them to do other projects."

However, although most FBO staff members reported that they were not engaged in evangelism, two staff members explicitly stated that evangelism was one of their goals. Several other FBO staff members insisted they did not evangelize, and yet they described activities that many would categorize as evangelism. Karl, who mentioned that his organization receives substantial funding from the United States government, described his FBO's evangelic mission. "[Our NGO's] mission is relief and evangelism, even though in Sri Lanka the evangelism mandate is dealt with lightly due to the social dynamics that are present here right now. In the south there is a strong anti-Christian element with the Buddhist parties, and the national legislature is currently considering an anti-conversion bill, so things are tense for us. So [our NGO's] goal is to show God's love through action. We don't have any direct evangelistic campaign here."

Author: But in other countries where you work, would you be more direct about evangelizing people?

Yes, if the situation permits it then we can be more direct. But this varies on a country-by-country basis. We have to be careful of the social and religious context. In other countries we could talk to people more openly about the gospel, but not here. So in Sri Lanka we hope that those touched by our work will ask questions about our faith, and then want to learn more about Christian teachings. In that way, they open the door for us. But we really want to live our faith by helping people, all people, regardless of what they believe. Conversion is a need of the hour, but (our NGO) focuses on compassionate, unconditional relief.

Harsha insisted his organization does not evangelize, but explained how service recipients end up joining his church after receiving trauma counseling following the tsunami. "We don't do evangelism. But we always take care of the spiritual side of the person, and we did this during the trauma counseling, as part of the tsunami response. What we did is we shared Christ's love at the end of the counseling. Some people, they accepted Christ, and then their life is definitely changed. And now we have joined the people to our church, they are coming to Sunday services. And you can see the effects of it, because they have stopped drinking, they have stopped smoking, and so you can see a difference in their life, in the way they live, in how they take care of their house and take care of their children."

Author: "I'm curious, if you don't do any direct evangelism, what do you think makes the people start coming to your church?"

Well, some people they ask, "Why are you coming and doing this for us?" Then we share Christ's love, we say, "Christ loves us and we will show Christ's love to you through us." So this makes them understand what we're doing.

Author: "So usually they would ask you?"

Yes, because they are surprised. They think, "Why is this man doing things for us when he doesn't have to?" So they always have this question on their mind.

In contrast to more direct forms of evangelism, the dynamic that Harsha describes is a type of "lifestyle evangelism" that has been observed by researchers examining FBOs in other parts of the developing world. By living life in the manner of Christ, FBO staff members provide an example to community members and lead nonbelievers to Christianity by building relationships that cause community members to feel an affinity to the FBO. For many staff members engaged in lifestyle evangelism, their Christian behavior is not a concerted effort to allure adherents. Rather, staff members' faith is so interwoven with other aspects of their development work that the two are inseparable, and attracting new adherents is the unintended but welcome result of their daily work activities. However, whether or not such outcomes are intentional, important power differentials come into play in lifestyle evangelism. In these service contexts the referent power of FBO staff members, deriving from their ability to develop an interpersonal relationship of trust and empathy with service recipients, serves to persuade service recipients to change their behavior and perhaps to adopt a new faith. As will be discussed shortly, when combined with the power that organizations derive from their control of critical resources, the referent power used in lifestyle evangelism can cause service recipients to face a serious power disadvantage when seeking to meet their basic needs.[27]

The quotes above are included at length in order to demonstrate fully how some FBOs do in fact have a goal of evangelism, and engage in evangelism during service provision. While many accusations of evangelism by FBOs are undoubtedly false, it seems that fears of conversion in Sri Lanka are not entirely unfounded. Highly publicized incidents of FBOs engaging in conversion, particularly post-tsunami, have given Sri Lankans a negative perception of the FBO community at large and unquestionably make it more difficult for FBOs to conduct their work.[28]

Implications for Inclusion, Exclusion, and Coercion

In Lebanon, the clearly sectarian nature of service provision presented an ideal environment for exclusion from services. In Sri Lanka, the potential for exclusion from service provision is less clear. According to NGO staff members, most service provision by FBOs and secular NGOs alike is inclusive, representing the multitude of religious and ethnic groups living in the area. However, in spite of the fact that most FBOs report serving diverse recipients, there are still factors in NGO service provision in Sri Lanka that can lead to exclusion in service provision and—perhaps more important— to evangelistic coercion in service provision.

One potentially exclusionary aspect of service provision by FBOs in Sri Lanka is the high degree of reliance on referrals from local religious bodies when selecting service recipients. A number of staff members from Buddhist, Christian, and "spiritual" FBOs indicated that their organizations used religious referrals as one way of selecting service recipients. The staff members from Buddhist and "spiritual" FBOs explicitly mentioned accepting referrals from any religious body, including churches, Buddhist and Hindu temples, and mosques. This was particularly the case in terms of tsunami aid, where referrals from a religious body, regardless of the religion, were seen as one way of ensuring that the aid was truly needed and that claims of lost property were legitimate. However, participants from Christian FBOs typically only mentioned accepting referrals from local churches.

It is important to note that none of the staff members indicated that referral from religious bodies was their organization's *sole* means of selecting service recipients. FBOs and NGOs normally also selected clients on the basis of referrals from local government authorities, village social service committees, and their own needs assessments. In many cases, however, local religious leaders were used to verify the legitimacy of claims for aid. George explains: "People knew that the church would respond, so they came up to the priest and they gave letters saying they needed help buying a bike or they needed help with food for their child. So they got lots of those letters, and the clergy would compile a list and send us a request and we would send them the money. Or, there were local officials, government officials, who would express a need to do this or that. In both cases someone from the clergy would verify that this was a real need, replacing things people had really lost. So this was also a way of not wasting money, of using money where it was most needed."

This reliance on religious bodies for referrals and on religious leaders to check the veracity of requests for aid has the potential to exclude individuals in need who (a) are not known to local religious leaders of the faith group providing aid, (b) are not members of a specific religious community, or (c) may not feel comfortable approaching religious leaders (perhaps especially those from a different religion) for help. Given the widespread public fear of conversion in Sri Lanka, individuals in need may be particularly apprehensive about approaching Christian leaders for assistance. Also problematic is the fact that Christian FBOs were highly reliant on local churches as a location for service provision; more than 75 percent of staff members from Christian FBOs indicated that they used churches as a site for service delivery on at least some occasions.

Cara, a staff member from a Christian FBO explained that "The difference in a sense here is that lots of the work is being done directly through churches, but it is being given to everyone regardless, so the beneficiaries are anybody, and they certainly aren't all Christians, or congregations of churches, or whatever." Cara did not seem to see the provision of aid through churches as potentially exclusionary. However, it is easy to imagine that non-Christians who might not understand that services are open to everyone, or who might fear proselytization, would choose to avoid seeking services in churches. Thus a type of self-exclusion may result, and non-Christian members of the population may have less access to aid.

Another important exception to FBO reports of inclusive service provision is Muslim FBOs, who reported that they served an almost exclusively Muslim clientele. As will be discussed in the next section, sole service provision exacerbates the potential for exclusion, and in the case of Muslim FBOs, exclusion would occur if a Muslim FBO were to be the sole provider of a much-needed service in a multiethnic or multireligious locale. On the surface the Muslim FBO community in Sri Lanka seems to be quite small, overshadowed by numerous Christian FBOs and a few large and powerful Buddhist organizations, so the potential implications of this exclusive service provision are unclear.

Sole Service Provision by FBOs

Much as in Lebanon, in Sri Lanka a large number of NGOs report that they are the sole provider of certain services in their community. In fact, 100 percent of the staff members in Sri Lanka indicated that in some communities their NGO was the sole provider of certain services. This seems to be the result of a concerted effort to create a highly coordinated system of aid following the 2004 tsunami, particularly in the wake of scandals reported in the media involving the uncoordinated nature of the initial tsunami response and the accompanying wasted resources. All staff members indicated that their NGO was a member of councils that coordinated provision of services in various regions of the country. Therefore, it seems that NGOs tend to be sole service providers not because there are no other capable service providers in the region but as a consequence of intentional efforts not to duplicate services.[29] As Samanthi explains, "We are the only ones who are working in that area, because we don't want to duplicate the same thing over and over again that is already provided by other organizations. So before we go we will see what other organizations are working and what kind of work they are doing. If they are doing a certain kind of work then we won't do the same thing, we will do something else."

Even though NGOs reportedly are inclusive in their service provision, sole service provision by the majority of service providers gives NGOs a significant amount of power in comparison to their service recipients. Social service providers control critical resources that are needed by service recipients, and the amount of power a social service provider has over the service recipient is directly tied to the client's ability to obtain aid elsewhere. When organizations have a monopoly over services—a situation that is common in the global north and even more widespread in the developing world—they wield considerable power over service recipients. This power differential means that service recipients may be susceptible to coercion by NGO staff, and as a result, the coercive power of FBO sole service providers becomes problematic.[30]

As was discussed in Chapter 1, simply possessing a power advantage does not necessarily mean that power will be used at the expense of the service recipient. The use of power is governed by values and norms that include an organization's rules and regulations and the norms and ethics of one's profession. Whereas in the global north a culture of human services professionalism prevails in the nonprofit sector, in developing and transitional countries less public funding is available to NGOs, and reliance on voluntary labor is high. This heavy reliance on a volunteer workforce may increase the likelihood of philanthropic amateurism in the developing world, with services provided by those whom a moral or religious calling motivates rather than by professionals. The majority of staff members indicated that they had past professional training or past professional experience in health and social services, but it is difficult to know whether professional training in the developing world emphasizes respect for service recipients' rights not to be proselytized.

In addition, professional socialization may be overcome by organizational or religious imperatives to witness one's faith. Although the majority of FBO staff members reported that they do not engage in evangelism, those who do may put service recipients in the uncomfortable position of either complying with FBOs' religious efforts or excluding themselves from services. For those in desperate need of services, particularly war-affected or tsunami-affected individuals, this "choice" simply may not exist. The stark absence of choice becomes especially apparent when few if any alternative service providers exist.[31]

It is true that exclusion structured along religious lines does not seem to be as strong a risk in Sri Lanka as in Lebanon, but there certainly are a number of steps that could be taken to reduce the risk of exclusion from services. Moreover, in Sri Lanka an even greater concern seems to be potential coercion in service provision, particularly by Christian FBOs. Exclusionary and coercive behavior by NGOs has important implications not only for individuals' access to services that meet their basic human needs, but also for building trust across religious and ethnic communities and social institutions. A number of practical proposals for avoiding exclusionary and coercive activity are discussed in Chapter 5.

Notes

1. For more on the nature and causes of ethnic violence in Sri Lanka, see Neil DeVotta, *Blowback: Linguistic Nationalism, Institutional Decay, and Ethnic Conflict in Sri Lanka* (Stanford, CA: Stanford University Press, 2004). For more on the LTTE, and in particular on their innovations in suicide bombing, see Christopher Reuter, *My Life Is a Weapon: A Modern History of Suicide Bombing* (Princeton, NJ: Princeton University Press, 2002).

2. For more on Sri Lanka's voluntary sector, see Neil DeVotta, "Civil Society and Non-governmental Organizations in Sri Lanka: Peacemakers or Parasites?" *Civil Wars* 7, no. 2 (2005): 171–82; Camilla Orjuela, "Civil Society in Civil War: The Case of Sri Lanka," *Civil Wars* 7, no. 2 (2005): 120–37; and Ranjith Wanigaratne, "The State-NGO Relationship in Sri Lanka: Rights, Interests, and Accountability," in *NGOs, States and Donors: Too Close for Comfort?* ed. David Hulme and Michael Edwards (London: Macmillan Press, 1997).

3. For more information on the history of the Tamils in Sri Lanka, see A. Jeyaratnam Wilson, *Sri Lankan Tamil Nationalism: Its Origins and Development in the Nineteenth and Twentieth Centuries* (Vancouver: University of British Columbia Press, 2000).

4. For more on discrimination and subsequent radicalization in Sri Lanka, see A. J. V. Chandrakanthan, "Eelam Tamil Nationalism: An Inside View," in *Sri Lankan Tamil Nationalism: Its Origins and Development in the Nineteenth and Twentieth Centuries,* by A. Jeyaratnam Wilson (Vancouver: University of British Columbia Press, 2000); DeVotta, 2004; Chelvadurai Manogaran, *Ethnic Conflict and Reconciliation in Sri Lanka* (Honolulu: University of Hawaii Press, 1987); and Reuter, 2002.

5. DeVotta, 2004; Manogaran, 1987.

6. For more information on the LTTE's expulsion of Muslims from the north and east of Sri Lanka, see United States Department of State, *International Religious Freedom Report 2005* (Washington, DC: United States Department of State, 2005); and Laura Watkins, "Misreading Needs: The Question of Capacity Building and Local Participation Among Displaced Muslim Women in Puttalam District," *Civil Wars* 7, no. 2 (2005): 138–55. The quotation in this paragraph comes from an interview conducted in August 2006 in Colombo, Sri Lanka, with a scholar studying ethnic identity. Just as with my NGO interview participants, I offered this scholar a guarantee of anonymity prior to the interview.

7. DeVotta, 2005; Orjuela, 2005; Wanigaratne, 1997.

8. DeVotta, 2005.

9. DeVotta, 2005.

10. Orjuela, 2005; Wanigaratne, 1997.

11. For more on the perception of NGOs as corrupt, wasteful, and a threat to the state, see DeVotta, 2005; Roland Hodson, "Elephant Loose in the Jungle: The World Bank and NGOs in Sri Lanka," in *NGOs, States and Donors: Too Close for Comfort?* ed. David Hulme and Michael Edwards (London: Macmillan Press, 1997).

12. For more on perceptions of relationships between NGOs and the LTTE, see DeVotta, 2005; and Michael Renner, *Politicization of Aid*

in Sri Lanka Turns Deadly (Washington, DC: Worldwatch Institute, 2006).

13. For more on evangelism and expression of faith in service delivery in the United States, see Nancy T. Ammerman, *Doing Good in American Communities: Congregations and Service Organizations Working Together* (Hartford, CT: Hartford Institute for Religious Research, 2001); John P. Bartkowski, *The Promise and Peril of Charitable Choice: Faith-Based Initiatives in Mississippi* (Cambridge, MA: Harvard University Press, 2001); Alvia Y. Branch, *Faith and Action: Implementation of the National Faith-Based Initiative for High-Risk Youth* (Philadelphia, PA: Public/Private Ventures, 2002); Stephen V. Monsma and Carolyn M. Mounts, *Working Faith: How Religious Organizations Provide Welfare-to-Work Services* (Philadelphia, PA: Center for Religion and Urban Civil Society, 2002); and Jo Anne Schneider, Katie Day, and Gwynneth Anderson, *Connections Between Faith Communities and Their Non-profits. Findings from the Faith and Organizations Project Pilot Study* (Washington, DC: George Washington Institute for Public Policy, 2005). For more on evangelism and expression of faith in service delivery in the developing world, see Tamsin Bradley, "Does Compassion Bring Results? A Critical Perspective on Faith and Development," *Culture and Religion* 6, no. 3 (2005): 337–51; Shawn Teresa Flanigan, "Paying for God's Work: A Rights-Based Examination of Faith-Based NGOs in Romania," *VOLUNTAS: International Journal of Voluntary and Nonprofit Organizations* 18, no. 2 (2007): 156–75; and Sarah White and Romy Tiongco, *Doing Theology and Development: Meeting the Challenge of Poverty* (Edinburgh: Saint Andrew Press, 1997). For more on service recipients' perceptions of faith in social service settings, see Rebecca Sager and Laura Susan Stephens, "Serving Up Sermons: Clients' Reaction to Religious Elements at Congregation-Run Feeding Establishments," *Nonprofit and Voluntary Sector Quarterly* 34, no. 3 (2005): 297–315; and Schneider, Day, and Anderson, 2005.

14. United States Department of State, 2005; Wanigaratne, 1997.

15. For more on anti-conversion legislation in Sri Lanka, see Parliament of Sri Lanka, *A Bill on Prohibition of Forcible Conversion of*

Religions (Colombo: Parliament of Sri Lanka, 2004); and United States Department of State, 2005.

16. DeVotta, 2005; United States Department of State, 2005; Wanigaratne, 1997.

17. Parliament of Sri Lanka, 2004, p. 1.

18. United States Department of State, 2005.

19. Although efforts were made to select staff members in such a way as to reflect the religious diversity of the population, there are important limitations to the interviews conducted in Sri Lanka. Most important, no staff members from Hindu organizations were interviewed. Because of the escalating violence in Sri Lanka during the period of fieldwork (August 2006), and especially the execution of seventeen aid workers employed by an international NGO, in practice the military limited the ability of foreign nationals to travel to the north of the island, where Sri Lanka's Hindu population is concentrated. NGO staff members from a number of NGOs operating programs in the north of the country were conducted, by phone and also in person, because a large number of NGO staff normally working in the north of the island had been relocated to the south in response to security concerns. However, none of these staff members were from organizations that were explicitly Hindu.

20. For more on the secularization of international Christian FBOs, see Rachel M. McCleary and Robert J. Barro, "Private Voluntary Organizations Engaged in International Assistance, 1939–2004," *Nonprofit and Voluntary Sector Quarterly* 37, no. 3 (2008): 512–36; and Rachel McCleary, *Internationalizing American Compassion: The United States Government and Private Voluntary Agencies in International Relief and Development, 1939 to Present* (Oxford, England: Oxford University Press, 2009).

21. Bradley, 2005; Mark Chaves and William Tsitsos, "Congregations and Social Services: What They Do, How They Do It, and with Whom," *Nonprofit & Voluntary Sector Quarterly* 30, no. 4 (2001): 660–83; Helen Rose Ebaugh, Paula F. Pipes, Janet Saltzman Chafetz, and Martha Daniels, "Where's the Religion? Distinguishing Faith-Based

from Secular Social Service Agencies," *Journal for the Scientific Study of Religion* 42, no. 3 (2003): 411–26; Robert Fischer, "In God We Trust, All Others Bring Data: Assessing the State of Outcomes Measurement for Faith-Based and Community-Based Programming," in *Innovations in Effective Compassion: Compendium of Research Papers Presented at the Faith-Based and Community Initiatives Conference on Research, Outcomes, and Evaluation* (Washington, DC: US Department of Health and Human Services, 2008): 179–211; Byron R. Johnson, Ralph Brett Tompkins, and Derek Webb, *Objective Hope—Assessing the Effectiveness of Faith-Based Organizations: A Review of the Literature* (Philadelphia: University of Pennsylvania, Center for Research on Religion and Urban Civil Society, 2002).

22. Orjuela, 2005. Byron R. Johnson, Tompkins, and Webb, 2002.

23. For more on Christian theology and development, see Erica Borstein, "Developing Faith: Theologies of Economic Development in Zimbabwe," *Journal of Religion in Africa* 32, no.1 (2002): 4–31; Kirsteen Kim, *Concepts of Development in the Christian Traditions: A Religions and Development Background Paper, Working Paper No. 16* (Birmingham, England: Religions and Development Research Programme, University of Birmingham, 2007); and White and Tiongco, 1997. For more on Buddhist philosophy on development, see George D. Bond, *Buddhism at Work: Community Development, Social Empowerment and the Sarvodaya Movement* (West Hartford, CT: Kumarian Press, 2004); Kamla Chowdry and Wendy R. Tyndale, "The Sarvodaya Shramadana Movement," in *Visions of Development: Faith Based Initiatives,* ed. Wendy R. Tyndale (Aldershot, England: Ashgate Publishing Limited, 2006), 9–16; Joanna Macy, *Dharma and Development: Religion as Resource in the Sarvodaya Self-Help Movement* (West Hartford, CT: Kumarian Press, 1985); and White and Tiongco, 1997.

24. Jeevan Thiagarajah and Norbert Ropers, *An Annotation to the "Principles of Conduct for the International Federation of Red Cross and Red Crescent Societies/International Committee of the Red Cross and NGOs in Disaster Response Programmes"* (Colombo: Consortium

of Humanitarian Agencies and Berghof Foundation for Conflict Studies–Sri Lanka Office, 2005).

25. For more on the politicization of the religious and ethnic distribution of aid, see Renner, 2006; and Thiagarajah and Ropers, 2005.

26. For more on recruiting adherents as a possible goal of FBOs, see Helmut Anheier and Lester Salamon, *The Nonprofit Sector in the Developing World* (Manchester, England: Manchester University Press, 1998); Estelle James, *The Nonprofit Sector in International Perspective: Studies in Comparative Culture and Policy* (New York: Oxford University Press, 1989); and Susan Rose-Ackerman, "Altruism, Nonprofits and Economic Theory," *Journal of Economic Literature* 34, no. 2 (1996): 701–26. For more on perceptions of FBO evangelism in Sri Lanka, see Thiagarajah and Ropers, 2005. For more on the role of power in service provision, see Yeheskel Hasenfeld, *Human Service Organizations* (Englewood Cliffs, NJ: Prentice-Hall, 1983); and Yeheskel Hasenfeld, "Power in Social Work Practice," *Social Service Review* 61, no. 3 (1987): 469–83.

27. For more on lifestyle evangelism, see Erica Borstein, 2002. For more on the role of referent power in service provision, see Hasenfeld, 1987.

28. For more on reports of conversion in tsunami aid, see Thiagarajah and Ropers, 2005.

29. For more on post-tsunami scandals involving wasted aid, see DeVotta, 2005.

30. Hasenfeld, 1987.

31. For more on the role of power in service provision, see Hasenfeld, 1987. For more on the structure of the nonprofit labor force in the developing world, see Lester Salamon, S. Wojciech Sokolowski, and Regina List, *Global Civil Society: An Overview* (Baltimore, MD: Johns Hopkins Center for Civil Society Studies, 2003). For more on philanthropic amateurism, see Salamon, 1995.

4

Cities of Cemeteries

Legacies of Ethnic Cleansing in Bosnia and Herzegovina's NGO Sector

Bosnia and Herzegovina is one of several states that emerged with the fall of the former Yugoslavia in the 1990s. It is situated in south-eastern Europe and bordered by Croatia, Montenegro, and Serbia, with a small piece of coastline along the Adriatic Sea. In recent years the name *Bosnia and Herzegovina* brings to mind images of Serb campaigns of "ethnic cleansing" that displaced millions of people in the early 1990s. With hundreds of thousands of civilians killed, the conflict left the hillsides of Bosnia and Herzegovina's cities littered with a patchwork of cemeteries.

In the face of the humanitarian disaster of the war, a large number of international NGOs began to operate in Bosnia and Herzegovina, as well as elsewhere in the region. The end of communism in the former Yugoslavia created a new civic space for voluntary associations and nonprofit organizations, and in response to the great needs created by the war, many local social service NGOs began to emerge in Bosnia and Herzegovina as well. These include secular service providers and faith-based service providers from Bosnia and Herzegovina's multiple religious communities.

Violence in Bosnia and Herzegovina
and Ethno-religious Identity

Bosnia and Herzegovina's population of 4.5 million is composed of three dominant ethnicities: 48 percent Bosniak, 37.1 percent Serb, and 14.3 percent Croat. Other ethnicities make up 0.6 percent of the population. The central ethnic marker distinguishing these groups is their religious tradition. Serbs are traditionally Eastern Orthodox, Croats are normally Roman Catholic, and Bosniaks identify with Sunni Islam. Ethnicity and religious identity are considered so closely tied that the ethnic label *Bosniak* was coined specifically for Bosnia and Herzegovina's Muslim community, although in actuality Bosniaks are ethnically Slav, just as Serbs and Croats are. As some scholars of the region explain, religion and ethnicity are so intertwined that those who have converted from Christianity to Islam are perceived not only as having changed their religion but as having changed their race as well. The label *Bosniak* was accepted chiefly because Muslims in Bosnia and Herzegovina are largely secular, defined as Muslim by culture and tradition rather than by religious belief or practice. Therefore, *Bosniak* has replaced *Muslim* as an ethnic term in part to avoid confusion with practicing adherents of Islam.[1]

Bosnia and Herzegovina's ethnic communities and religious communities are quite closely aligned demographically. Muslims make up 40 percent of the population, Orthodox Christians constitute 31 percent, and Roman Catholics make up 15 percent of the population. Other religions make up 14 percent of the population, which includes a very small Jewish community and a growing population of Protestant Christians. Administratively the country is also divided along ethnic lines. Within Bosnia and Herzegovina's borders, the Bosniak/Croat Federation makes up about 51 percent of the territory, and the Bosnian Serb-led Republika Srpska makes up about 49 percent of the territory.[2]

The former Yugoslavia was a federation of eight federal units, including the six republics of Serbia, Croatia, Bosnia and Herzegovina, Slovenia, Macedonia, and Montenegro, as well as two autonomous provinces inside Serbia: Kosovo and Vojvodina. Only Slovenia could be considered effectively ethnically homogeneous; the other five of the six republics were inhabited primarily by the ethnic group for which they were named. The exception to this was Bosnia and Herzegovina, which was ethnically diverse with no single majority group. Some scholars assert that, given its ethnic diversity, violence was almost inevitable in Bosnia and Herzegovina once Yugoslavia began to split into independent, ethnically identified states. The civil war in the former Yugoslavia in the early 1990s was the worst eruption of violence in Europe since World War II. The conflict was characterized by mass rapes and other atrocities, and entire regions were devastated. Approximately a quarter of a million people died, and millions of people became refugees.[3]

This conflict was not necessarily new. Intercommunal violence between the region's ethnic and religious groups has periodically erupted in the Balkans since the nineteenth century. However, in the former Yugoslavia, ethno-religious tensions were not high at the individual level, thanks in part to communist leader Josip Tito's efforts to promote brotherhood and a unified Yugoslav identity above all others. When he felt it necessary, Tito suppressed nationalist movements that threatened to get out of hand, such as those in Croatia and Kosovo in the late 1960s and early 1970s. By the time Tito died in 1980, tensions were relatively low and intermarriage in ethnically mixed areas was high and on the rise. However, nationalist ideas were far from dead, and after Tito's death Yugoslavia's central institutions were too weak to handle these divisions.[4]

Even if the central government had been stronger, it is questionable whether the will existed to prevent these ethno-religious divisions. On the contrary, violent confrontation between ethnic groups occurred because political leaders in the various republics (in particular Serbia's Slobodan Milosevic) purposely fueled animosity between groups. This was done in an effort to build ruling coalitions by making Yugoslavs of other ethnicities scapegoats for the problems of their own populations. The steep decline of Yugoslavia's economy in the 1980s and the uneven development of the different republics made the population particularly susceptible to this rhetoric. Serbs' and Croats' national myths also fueled this tension. Members of each ethnic group were encouraged to perceive themselves as distinctively worthy, while ethnic political leaders underscored their own groups' uniquely disadvantaged position within the Yugoslav state. Prior to beginning the campaign of ethnic cleansing, Serb forces took control of the media in Bosnia and Herzegovina and mounted a publicity campaign intended to heighten Serb fears that they were under threat of extermination by Muslims and Croats. This and other tactics aimed at increasing fear among the general population offered militias a way to "legitimize the atrocities they committed.[5]

Serbia's ethnic cleansing policies in Bosnia and Herzegovina were applied through an assortment of means, including systematic mass murder, torture, mass deportation of civilians, and internment in detention or concentration camps. Also infamous was the practice of systematically raping and impregnating women and girls in an effort to produce "cleansed" and purified Serbian babies. These traumatizing acts ensured that many of those who survived the war would be opposed to returning to their homes even after the conflict ended. As of 2005, more than 10,000 refugees remained outside Bosnia and Herzegovina, and more than 180,000 people were internally displaced, remaining within the borders of Bosnia and Herzegovina but living outside their prewar communities.[6]

The Salience of Religion in the Ethnic Cleansing Campaign

Some scholars characterize nationalism in the former Yugoslavia as religious nationalism, in which fundamentalist versions of Christianity and nationalism strengthen each other and become one. But although they acknowledge that religious identity is crucially important to understanding the conflict in Bosnia and Herzegovina, most scholars characterize it as an ethnic conflict. Nevertheless, much as in Sri Lanka, ethnicity and religion in Bosnia and Herzegovina are so intertwined that a religious dimension clearly emerged during the conflict.[7]

Nationalists used religious symbolism to both encourage and defend the use of violence. Much of the violence within Bosnia and Herzegovina targeted mosques and churches, and outside actors supported those with whom they shared religious ties. Sites of religious significance were methodically destroyed, and many crimes (such as rape) were systematically perpetrated against certain religious communities (such as Muslim women). Milosevic allied himself with the Serbian Orthodox Church, favoring the Orthodox Church in public policy, providing government assistance for church reconstruction, and replacing Marxism with religious education in public schools. Government-controlled media went so far as to claim that Orthodox Christianity was the most critical element of Serb national identity.[8]

At different times both Croatian and Serbian nationalists attempted to portray the conflict as one between Christianity and Islam. Serbian nationalists described those who supported the Bosnian government as Islamic fundamentalists or "Khomeinis," whereas Croats blamed fighting on radical "mujahideen."[9] Politicians in both Croatia and Serbia rallied against a Bosnian state by stoking their followers' fears of an Islamic government akin to that of Iran emerging in the heart of Europe. For its part, Bosnia and Herzegovina initially was eager to portray itself to the West as a victim of ethnic cleansing and the sole multiethnic combatant in the breakup of Yugoslavia. However, as the war went on, domestic and international dynamics pushed Islam to the forefront, and Bosnia and Herzegovina increasingly sought aid from Middle Eastern countries. The war itself radicalized Bosnia and Herzegovina's population and increased interest in Islam, transforming many secular Bosniaks into practicing Muslims. As is evident here, even though the conflict in Bosnia and Herzegovina was not directly related to religious belief, religious identity nonetheless played an important role.[10]

Religion, Violence, and the NGO Sector in Bosnia and Herzegovina

In both Lebanon and Sri Lanka, the NGO sector evolved in part from the diverse faith communities present in each country and their traditions of philanthropy and service to the poor. The result is that both countries have a relatively large and active community of local FBOs. The same cannot be said of Bosnia and Herzegovina. Each of the three primary religious communities in Bosnia and Herzegovina has a single dominant faith-based social service organization, and in some instances a few other small local FBOs have emerged in the same faith community. However, the scope and scale of the local FBO community are quite small when compared to many other countries, particularly the countries discussed in this book. Instead, the FBO community in Bosnia and Herzegovina is composed primarily of international FBOs that arrived in the region to provide aid during and after the war. This difference in the development of the FBO sector in Bosnia and Herzegovina can be attributed to Yugoslavia's fifty years of communist rule, as well as to the war itself.[11]

In many parts of Central and Eastern Europe, an era of Soviet-style communism destroyed a tradition of civic engagement and political representation that had existed during previous periods. Yugoslavia was the leader of a number of "nonaligned" countries that did not give their allegiance to the Soviet Union, and Tito pursued his own anti-Stalinist, Western-oriented form of socialism that led to greater prosperity in Yugoslavia than in much of the communist world. Tito did not repress associational activity and religious life to the same extent that many other communist leaders did, but restrictions still remained. Religious activity was a private affair that was confined to people's homes and carefully hidden from public view. Meanwhile, those civic associations that existed were state-sponsored groups such as trade unions, cultural associations, and sporting clubs. With the notable exception of the International Red Cross, NGOs that provided for social service needs, particularly religious NGOs, did not exist.[12] As Amir, an NGO staff member, explains, "I think a big reason it is difficult to find a lot of local faith-based NGOs is that many of these organizations didn't exist during the socialist time. Sometimes they were outlawed, or also often there just wasn't a need because the government took care of all those things, all the social needs were met by the state."

In its short history, however, Bosnia and Herzegovina's NGO sector has become quite large. Depending on the source of information, the number of NGOs in Bosnia and Herzegovina is estimated at several hundred to several thousand. Although the term *NGO* is commonly used throughout country, that designation does not exist legally, and any such organization is instead registered with the government either as an "association of citizens" or as a "foundation." Because there is no distinction among the types of associations, it is difficult to estimate how many of them are engaged in providing services to beneficiaries. The International Council of Voluntary Agencies estimates that approximately 39 percent of the associations of citizens registered with various government ministries in Bosnia and Herzegovina have developmental and humanitarian aims.[13]

Bosnia and Herzegovina's NGO sector emerged not only because of a new government system that was more open to civic association. Many health and social service NGOs were created as a direct response to the needs produced by the war. In fact, three-quarters of the NGO staff members interviewed for this book indicated that their NGO had begun its activities in Bosnia and Herzegovina in response to the aftermath of the war. Because of this, many participants indicated that their NGOs have adopted an explicitly antireligious or multireligious identity. As Tatjana puts it, "Before the war, there were citizen associations, but these were more for sports and culture, but not NGOs providing services to people like in the Western world. So the NGOs came with the war, we were established as a result of the war, most of us. And because of that, we don't want to be religious, and we don't want anything to do with any national group. We saw the bad things that brings, and we have to deal with those bad things in our work, still today. So if we are with a religion we would have to say we are with every religion, every nation."

In stark contrast to Lebanon and Sri Lanka, where many FBOs emerged from society's rich religious traditions, in Bosnia and Herzegovina many NGOs have emerged in response to the aftermath of ethno-religious conflict and, if anything, would like to distance themselves from religion as much as possible. However, this is not to say that there is not an active FBO sector in Bosnia and Herzegovina. There is a large community of international FBOs in the country, as well as a small group of local FBOs. Some staff from local Orthodox and Muslim FBOs explained that they had existed before communism, only to close their operations and then reopen fifty years later. Mirjana explains: "We existed before the Second World War, we even existed in the 1800s, but we stopped when communism came because they stopped all those sorts of organizations. But then after the war there were lots of problems and one priest said he remembered there used to be this kind of organization that helped people, so maybe we should start it again. And I said okay, me and the other ladies, we will start again. So we don't consider that we are new. We are just continuing that work from old times."

The Role of Faith in Social Service NGOs in Bosnia and Herzegovina

As was just discussed, the FBO sector in Bosnia and Herzegovina is small compared to that in Lebanon and in Sri Lanka, and many NGOs have adopted an explicitly secular identity. As a result, less than one-quarter of NGO staff interviewed in Bosnia and Herzegovina worked for FBOs. As in Sri Lanka, some staff mentioned that although their organization had faith origins, it now operated as a secular organization. However, only two individuals made note of this. Therefore, secularization seems to be much less prominent among FBOs in Bosnia and Herzegovina than among FBOs in Sri Lanka, where 40 percent of staff members from FBOs indicated that their organization had become secular over time.

Working in the NGO Sector: Community, Faith, and War

In previous chapters, the role of faith in leading staff members to a career in the nonprofit sector is considered an important indicator of the salience of religious identity for NGO staff. Much as in Lebanon and Sri Lanka, personal ties within particular religious communities played an important role in leading many FBO staff to work for their organization. Almost two-thirds of all staff members from FBOs mentioned that their personal ties within a particular religious community had led them to work for their FBO. Just as in Lebanon and Sri Lanka, these personal ties typically involved a member of their religious congregation informing them of the availability of the job and referring them to the individual responsible for hiring. In the case of one interfaith FBO, staff members had been nominated to their positions by leaders of their respective faith communities. In addition to the participants from this interfaith FBO, interview participants from Orthodox FBOs were most likely to indicate that they had come to work for their organization through personal ties they had within their religious community.

Again as in Lebanon and Sri Lanka, in Bosnia and Herzegovina a number of staff members explained their career path with stories about religious belief and religious inspiration. Staff members from Muslim FBOs were most likely to indicate that religious belief or religious inspiration was one of the factors that drew them to work for the organization. This is quite different from staff from Muslim FBOs in Sri Lanka, whose organizations had become highly secularized over time. In contrast to interview participants from Muslim FBOs in Lebanon, who often gave examples of teachings from the Koran to explain their work, interview participants from Muslim FBOs spoke of more general obligations to help humankind and promote positive behavior. As Fadila explains, "As Muslims we do feel some kind of obligation to use the best motives and principles from our religion to help human beings, and we really try to be transparent with this. We want to promote good things in life generally, for example not to use alcohol or drugs or do anything bad. We want to talk to people about this, and of course this is from our religion."

One staff member from a Catholic FBO and one staff member from a Protestant Christian FBO also mentioned the role that religious belief played in motivating their work. However, no staff from Orthodox FBOs mentioned religious belief as a motivator for their work.

It is interesting to note the relatively minor role that professional training and/or past professional experience in health and social services played in career choice by NGO staff in Bosnia and Herzegovina. When asked, "How did you personally come to work for this organization?" less than half of NGO staff indicated that their professional training and/or past professional experience in health and social services was one factor that led them to work for their NGO. This stands in contrast to the cases of Lebanon and Sri Lanka, where more than 75 percent of NGO staff who were interviewed came to their work through past professional training or experience. In Bosnia and Herzegovina, many NGO staff reported that they came to work for their NGO as a result of the aftermath of the war. Approximately one-third of the NGO staff who were interviewed indicated that this was one reason why they began working for their NGO, and many indicated that they had been professionally trained in fields not typically associated with health and social services, such as engineering or chemistry. The path that led them to work in the NGO sector normally took one of two forms. Some began working for NGOs as a result of high unemployment and an inability to find work in their own field (the newly present NGO sector was hiring with more frequency). Many interview participants then grew to love their jobs, as Nina did:

> To be honest I just really needed a job, and I didn't care where. But now I have seen that NGOs have power, and NGOs can influence politics and influence laws to protect children, or families. Political parties are not interested in these things. So NGOs pushed for laws on domestic violence, laws on gender equality, laws on family protection. These were some of our big successes as an NGO community. This is how I realized that working in NGOs is more interesting. You create something, and you push for something, and then you can see the changes and feel very proud of your work. This is why I will keep working with NGOs until my old age.

Others began their work as a consequence their own war experiences, particularly as refugees. Selma is an example: "When I returned from Germany, I really understood the difficult things about being a refugee, because I was a refugee myself. So when I returned to Bosnia and saw that so many displaced women are living in the collective centers, I thought I owed it to them to help them, the way the NGOs in Germany helped me. Of course I didn't know anything about this NGO work at that time. I just started doing some work for these women and then slowly we learned about how to become an NGO."

All those individuals who reported that they began working in the NGO sector as a result of the war worked with secular NGOs.

The Added Benefits of Faith

Just as in Lebanon and Sri Lanka, and as also reported in the literature on FBOs in the United States and the developing world, several FBO staff members in Bosnia and Herzegovina indicated that religious identity gives some form of added value to the services they provide.[14] Whereas in Sri Lanka less than half of the staff from FBOs felt that the religious orientation of their NGO added value to the services that they provide, in Bosnia and Herzegovina more than 70 percent of FBO staff reported that their faith increased the quality of their services. This is very similar to the percentage of FBO staff in Lebanon who perceived faith as adding value to their services. The staff members who indicated there was an added value to their work included all participants from Catholic, interfaith, and Muslim FBOs and two-thirds of staff members from Protestant Christian FBOs. The added value that staff members perceived faith as bringing to their organizations' work included

- more individualized and compassionate service provision
- more highly committed and motivated workers
- more effective service provision thanks to church networks
- more secure funding and more flexibility in use of funds
- ability to promote reconciliation through service provision

Some of these benefits, such as more individualized and compassionate service provision, and more highly committed and motivated workers, are often mentioned in the literature on FBOs in the United States and were also mentioned by interview participants from FBOs in Lebanon.

More effective service provision thanks to church networks, though not commonly mentioned in the US literature, was also mentioned by interview participants from FBOs in Sri Lanka. Two of these benefits were mentioned only by FBOs in Bosnia and Herzegovina: more secure funding and more flexibility in use of funds, and the ability to promote reconciliation between ethno-religious groups through service provision.

More Compassionate Service Provision

Three interview participants from Christian FBOs and two interview participants from Muslim FBOs mentioned more compassionate service provision as an added benefit that was derived from their religious orientation. This claim is often made by supporters of faith-based service provision in the global north, such as supporters of President George W. Bush's faith-based initiative in the United States.[15] Adrijana describes how Christian faith causes her FBO to be more compassionate toward people in need: "In terms of how we interact with the people, I cannot say the other NGOs are bad and we are the best. No. Everyone is giving very much. But somehow when you feel this in your heart, that this work is given to you by God, maybe you behave a bit different. Maybe your arms are a bit more open, and your heart is a bit more open."

Jasmina, a staff member from a Muslim FBO, indicated that she believes religion of any sort gives FBO employees more empathy for their service recipients. "I believe that religious NGOs have more benefits to give. I really believe that. Any organization that is a religious organization, in any religion, if someone who works there is really a person who believes in God in any way and is true to himself and what he believes, he must be a good person. So he must be more emotional, more empathic, because this is originally from religion."

More Motivated and Committed Workers

Another assertion often made in the United States context is that FBOs have more highly motivated workers and have access to a large pool of committed volunteers.[16] Just as in Lebanon, staff members from Christian and Muslim FBOs in Bosnia and Herzegovina indicated that they believed religious faith caused their workers to be more committed in the face of adversity. All of these interview participants indicated that the evidence of this increased commitment was that their staff worked for lower pay than staff of other organizations or were less motivated by money and prestige than staff of other organizations. As Amra, an interview participant from a Muslim FBO, explains,

> In other organizations that are not religious, you can see that people just work for money, or just work for some name or some special position in society, but I think in the religious NGOs the person doesn't work for money. He works because he believes God wants him to work like that, to help other people. For example, I just want God to give me a reward, I don't need it from people, and I can work hard and give all my knowledge and all my energy to this job. In all religious organizations, I believe it is like this, because I met some people who are Christians and they work in some organizations and I think they are like that too.

More Effective Service Provision
Thanks to Church Networks

Several staff members from Christian FBOs mentioned that they believed church networks enabled them to be more effective service providers. All of these interview participants were from international Catholic organizations. Much as in Sri Lanka, interview participants from international NGOs believed that churches gave them broader access to the community and provided them with partners who had intimate knowledge of their communities' needs. As Teresa explains, "It's wonderful because [the local Catholic NGO] has some grassroots networks, and we couldn't reach those people without those grassroots networks. So that is a real benefit to being a Catholic organization and having a Catholic partner, because they have those parish structures that can reach out to communities that we might not be able to reach out to otherwise. This gives us an advantage over some other foreign organizations who maybe come in and don't have any natural partner to work with as soon as they arrive."

More Secure and Flexible Funding

Another interesting benefit mentioned by several interview participants from Catholic FBOs and Protestant Christian FBO is that, because their funding comes from religious sources, they feel that their funds are more secure and that they can use them more flexibly. All but one of the interview participants who mentioned this benefit were from international FBOs. Patrick explains:

> We are fortunate that we are able to raise money from people in [our home country], many of whom are Catholic. That's a benefit that we get from being a Catholic organization, and we try to use that money wisely. It's nice, it gives us a little more flexibility. For example, my salary is paid by [our NGO], so I don't have to go out and fundraise for my salary. I can spend more time on things like partnerships with the local Catholic organizations instead of working solely on, for example, a reconstruction project funded by the Dutch government. I can allocate my time in a much more flexible manner, and we can put more of our donor money into the direct implementation of projects. It's a nice situation. There are some organizations that ran their projects here on grant money only, and so when their grant money ran out, they had to close their doors.

Ability to Promote Reconciliation Through Service Provision

A final benefit that interview participants from interfaith, international Catholic, Protestant Christian, and local Muslim FBOs mentioned was that they felt their religious identity enabled them to promote understanding and reconciliation between Bosnia and Herzegovina's different ethno-religious groups. Because the interfaith FBO had reconciliation as the main motivation of its founding, and its activities focused mostly on interfaith dialogue, with only a small component devoted to service provision, perhaps this is not surprising. Several staff members from Christian FBOs followed various forms of peace theology and therefore felt that peace building was inherent to their religion's teachings and their mission. However, the participants from Catholic and Muslim FBOs did not attribute opportunities for understanding and reconciliation to the teachings of their faith per se but, rather, to the fact that inclusive service provision and outreach to other communities could promote a positive image of their religious group. As Jacques, a staff member from a Catholic FBO, notes, "We as a faith-based organization are showing that we are not only working for the Catholics but also for the other groups, and I think this is something very special to show the people, that you don't only look at your own group but that you are trying to support people in need. Honestly I think that is one of the most important things we do here, just as important as the houses we rebuild or the aid we provide."

Although participants from Muslim FBOs spoke of the ways in which inclusive service provision could help promote greater understanding, they also spoke of the important role their FBO needed to play in improving impressions of Muslims in light of terror attacks in recent years. As Nermina explains,

> Sometimes there is prejudice about Muslims and if someone comes here for our help they might feel strange, but we just want to talk and explain. If anyone has any questions about Islam, we are open to talk about it, because this prejudice is something that is really a problem. You know, in the world generally people think bad about Islam because of all these terrorist attacks. But we just try to explain what are the rules of Islam, because of course every Muslim is not a good Muslim. We just want to show what things come from people, but don't come from Islam the religion. We have to make a [distinction] between bad people who happen to be Muslims and what they to do, and what is Islam really.

Staff members from Orthodox FBOs were the only FBO participants who did not see any added value from the religious orientation of their organization. This was the case even when interview participants were asked directly about any benefits they felt faith brought to their organization. As Sladjana, a staff member from an Orthodox FBO, puts it, "I don't know, I guess maybe faith might help. But mostly it is important that your parents raised you to be a good person, to want to help others. I mean, lots of religious people go to church every day but they don't ever help anyone. So faith, maybe it helps. But it is not really the important thing."

Religion as a Service Rendered

One interview participant from a Catholic FBO and two interview participants from Muslim FBOs also described religious services that their organizations provided. However, in contrast to the cases of Lebanon and Sri Lanka, these participants described only concrete, scheduled activities as opposed to moral and spiritual development. Participants from Muslim FBOs explained that their organizations offered courses on Islam and classes on the Koran for practicing Muslims, as well and introductory courses on Islam for non-Muslims and nonpracticing Muslims. These courses were available to those who chose to enroll and were not incorporated into other types of service provision. Jadranka, a staff member from a Catholic FBO, described masses held for FBO volunteers and also services provided by priests to the ill and to prisoners. As she explains,

> We also try to organize different spiritual exercises, meetings with the people talking about faith and how God can help us with certain activities. In certain projects we also have the assistance of priest within the projects, like for people who are sick at home or dying, and we have our missionary work in the hospitals and the prisons, the priests are going there. We try to implement the values of our faith inside of every activity. When it's possible we have masses, like on the Day of Volunteers we call the volunteers for a mass and then have a meeting. We try to involve this religious part. This makes us different than the other organizations.

Religious Identity and
Service Provision—Insiders and Outsiders

The interviews conducted in Bosnia and Herzegovina present an interesting illustration of polarization and boundary activation: local FBOs from Bosnia and Herzegovina's three primary faith communities provide services primarily to those of their own ethno-religious group, whereas international FBOs and secular NGOs are more inclusive in their service provision. All staff members from a local Catholic FBO, local Orthodox FBOs, and local Muslim FBOs indicated that the majority of the population they served belonged to their own religious group. Staff from an international Muslim FBO reported serving mostly Muslims as well. As can be seen here, the local FBOs whose ethnoreligious groups were involved in the war primarily serve members of their own group.

In contrast, all staff members from Protestant Christian FBOs, and by definition all staff members from interfaith FBOs, indicated that their organizations served ethnically and religiously mixed clientele. In addition, all but two staff members from secular NGOs indicated that they served ethnically and religiously mixed recipients. The two staff members who did not serve a mixed group of recipients worked with secular NGOs whose specific target population is the Roma (Gypsy) community, because this group is extremely marginalized within Bosnian society. The fact that secular NGOs in Bosnia and Herzegovina serve a mixed group of recipients stands in contrast to Lebanon, where many secular NGOs indicated that they served a single religious group as a consequence of their geographic location and the general geographic segregation of religious communities.

Most of the staff members who indicated that their FBOs serve primarily members of the same religious group stated that in Bosnia and Herzegovina, service recipients are most familiar with the service organization of their own religion and therefore feel most comfortable approaching those organizations for help. Of the staff members who indicated that their FBOs serve primarily members of the same religious group, more than half indicated that they were open to serving all people in need, regardless of their ethno-religious identity. As Emir explains, "This Muslim charitable society is not a prefix that means we should only help Muslims, just like [the Catholic NGO] should not only help Croats. Because this is a multireligious country, we are trying to help everyone, but it is true I cannot say this percentage is very high. It is true that most people we help are Muslims, but we never ask any name or religion, we don't ask anything."

Even though most interview participants from Orthodox FBOs did not indicate openness to helping members of other groups, Borislava notes, "It is true that our organization mostly serves Serbs, because since it is part of the Orthodox Church, the Serbs feel like it belongs to them. But we will serve anyone who comes for help. I remember in the beginning Muslims from the neighborhood sometimes came, and when we would ask their name they would be afraid, because their name is not a Serb name, so they would be afraid we would send them away. But we always helped them."

These interviews strongly support the argument that an FBO sharing the same ethnic and/or religious identity as one of the groups involved in violent conflict will serve fewer community members with a different ethno-religious identity. As can be seen here, the local FBOs whose ethno-religious groups were involved in the war primarily serve members of their own group, if not by their own intention then because the local community approaches only FBOs of their own faith. In contrast, international FBOs serve a more diverse group of service recipients. This is probably because they were not personally involved in the conflict. Because they do not have the sense that their community was personally affected by the war, they may feel more open to serving others. Furthermore, if service recipients see these FBOs as impartial "outsiders," they may be more comfortable approaching such organizations for help.

War-Affected or Unaffected: The Case of Catholic FBOs

All staff members from international Catholic FBOs mentioned the challenges they faced in working with the local Catholic community when they first arrived in Bosnia and Herzegovina. Whereas local Catholics felt that international Catholic FBOs should give priority to assisting the local Catholic community, these large and highly professionalized relief agencies had policies ensuring that they provided services on specific needs-based criteria. As Mary explains,

> We as a Catholic organization, we think that solidarity, justice and peace is something very important that is laid down in our faith. But

at the same time we are a modern humanitarian agency who has to provide quality services for the donors who provide money, and as you can see, our most important donors are government. So this is a challenge for us, and also sometimes a problem for our local Catholic partners, who sometimes are more inclined to focus on their own group. The Catholics had quite a difficult time here during the war, and many were driven out from Bosnia and Herzegovina and don't want to return. So we have had to work with the local Catholic partners so that they also have the understanding that we want to focus on the people in need, not focusing just on the Catholic community.

As Ellen observes, often the neediest in the community are not Catholics, but members of other groups. Ellen felt that helping those most in need regardless of religion was the most genuine expression of Catholic faith, but local Catholics often felt this violated the solidarity that international Catholics should share with their co-religionists.

We have to balance our Catholicism with our need to support those most in need, and I think sometimes the Catholic church here gets upset a bit because we are not seen as supporting more Catholics. We have to be very careful in the way that we work with them. It's a complicated relationship in a place like Bosnia, where there are many people in need but the majority of those in need are not Catholic. So that's really tough. It's complicated, and it's political. But at our very roots we have to live our faith by helping those most in need, and I think deep down our response is a Catholic response to the needs in Bosnia.

The Value of "Outsiders" Providing Services

A number of staff members, from both FBOs and secular NGOs, indicated that service provision could be much easier when recipients viewed providers as impartial and coming from outside the conflict. This was particularly true for international FBOs. FBOs of Protestant denominations that previously had never been heard of in Bosnia and Herzegovina often had an easier time gaining the trust of locals and of other religiously or ethnically identified organizations in the country. However, international Catholic organizations in particular had larger hurdles to jump when establishing themselves as inclusive service providers. As Magdalena notes,

> When we work with people, the first sentence we say is, "We work with minority returnees." And they say, "So you are supporting Croats," because we are Catholic. So then we have to say, "Okay, we are supporting Croats here, but we support Serbs here, and Bosniaks here. We support minorities, and in Bosnia everybody is a minority somewhere." But we became known in the field as an organization that is really working and helping according to the criteria of each project, so then they became comfortable with us. Now I think they don't even think about us that we are Catholic, they just think we are foreign, from outside.

It is important to note that FBOs are not the only organizations that face these sorts of tensions in service provision. Tensions often are present for secular providers as well, especially for Bosnian staff members. An interview participant from a secular NGO explains the value of being seen as an "outsider," even if only as an outsider in one particular village:

> We are always faced with the issue of being on this side or on the other side. Especially working in minority return, we always try to also work with another ethnic group. Then you, as someone who came from outside the community, if you succeed for people to trust in you, then you become some kind of a filter for them. Sometimes people from your own ethnic group will tell you something horrible that is difficult to hear or to understand. Also, when you work in a mixed village, people will tell you, "He shot at me during the war," and this is difficult to manage. So it is important that they see you as being from outside, not taking a side, even though you are from Bosnia.

Tensions for Bosnian Staff

As the quotation above demonstrates, tensions in service provision may become even more difficult for Bosnian staff members, most of whom have been personally affected by the war. Throughout the interviews, many Bosnian nationals made an effort to emphasize that the conflict in Bosnia and Herzegovina was based on political rather than personal differences. As Sabina explains, "You have to understand something. In Bosnia, before the war, during the war, and after the war, there was never really a problem between ordinary people. This was only a problem between politicians, and it was like that before the war, during the war, and it's like that now. We didn't do this; the politicians did this."

Nonetheless, individuals' personal lives were undoubtedly affected by the conflict in many ways, and naturally this has an effect on people's openness to each other and to each other's ideas regarding the social problems left by the war. A number of staff members told stories illustrating that these tensions had not affected relations with service recipients so much as with other staff members. This seemed to be the case particularly when coworkers from the Federation and from Republika Srpska gathered together. Many practical problems seemed to surround communication, such as the existence of "taboo" topics that were consciously avoided and drastically different interpretations of past events. These dynamics present a difficult problem for organizations that are working with war victims and therefore need to be able to discuss these topics openly. Emina explains how her colleagues avoid talking about the war:

> The divisions do cause us practical problems, especially because now in Republika Srpska we provide training to other professionals, and that is our biggest problem, because we as professionals still cannot talk openly about the war. It's professional training, so we talk about how to work with traumatized people, but how can we talk about how to talk with your traumatized patients about the war when we can't even talk about it ourselves? We consciously avoid that, because we think it is not the time now. And people have these small sentences, they talk about "my war" and "your war," like "My war was worse," as in my suffering was worse. We as a profession, we are not able to discuss it, so how do we expect ordinary people to communicate, people who were raped or tortured or lost their children?

Samir describes how different narratives of past events caused tensions during staff training that he was conducting:

I was doing my training and it was going really well. But then someone started talking about one concentration camp, this is a place where some huge massacres happened, I mean thousands of people died. And one man from that area, he said, "No, that wasn't a concentration camp." He said, "That was just a place where people were kept so they would be safe during the war until they could go home," and he said no one died there. I mean, these massacres have been documented by many international groups, there is no doubt that they happened. Thousands of bodies were found. Really. So what do you say to that? And some people in the training, they work with people whose family died in that camp. So what can they even say to something like that?

In a context such as Bosnia and Herzegovina, where people were so broadly affected by the war, we might be able to assume that ethnoreligious identity is highly salient for all Bosnian nationals. As a result, it cannot help but come to bear on one's perception of one's work, interaction with service recipients, and interaction with coworkers. As Ibrahim, a staff member from a Muslim FBO, so poignantly observed, "We are trying and I think we are successful with cooperation with others. I believe in general all Bosniaks are like this, open to others." Then, after a pause, "Well, a mother from Srebrenica[17] who saw her husband and sons killed, maybe she cannot feel that way yet."

Implications for Inclusion in and Exclusion from Services

The information from the interviews indicates that access to NGOs' social services in Bosnia and Herzegovina is largely inclusive, with less than one-fourth of staff members indicating they provided services primarily to their own ethno-religious group. For local FBOs from Bosnia and Herzegovina's three predominant religious communities, service provision is structured in such a way that the existing religious and ethnic divisions in Bosnian society are duplicated by the NGO social service system. This dynamic is quite similar to that found among NGO service providers in Lebanon, but the risk of exclusion is tempered by the large number of international NGOs and local secular NGOs that provide services in Bosnia and Herzegovina.

Although the interviews indicated that referrals from other religiously identified organizations were one means by which NGOs select whom they will serve, religious referrals seem to play much less of a role in Bosnia and Herzegovina than in Lebanon and Sri Lanka. One staff member from a Catholic FBO and all staff from Orthodox FBOs indicated that they used religious referrals as one way of selecting service recipients, and they all accepted referrals from local churches within their own denomination. It is interesting to note that in Lebanon, Sri Lanka, and Bosnia and Herzegovina alike, Christian FBOs seem to be more likely to rely on religious referrals than are FBOs of other faiths.

Sole Service Provision

Much like Sri Lanka, Bosnia and Herzegovina seems to have a large number of organizations that are the sole providers of services; more than 80 percent of staff members indicated that they were the sole providers of certain services in some communities. This included interview participants from Catholic, Protestant Christian, interfaith, and Muslim FBOs, as well as participants from secular NGOs. As in Sri Lanka, some staff mentioned that this was largely due to a coordinated and concerted effort on the part of the NGO community to avoid duplicating the services of other NGOs. This coordination seems to have begun during the war when international NGOs began providing humanitarian aid.

However, the fact that a large percentage of NGOs are sole service providers may have few implications for exclusion from services. The only staff members who indicated that they serve primarily their own religious group and are also the sole providers of certain services were staff members from Muslim FBOs. The other staff members from FBOs who indicated that their organizations were sole providers of some services were from international FBOs that reportedly are inclusive in their service provision. Admittedly, if Muslim FBOs are the sole providers of a highly needed service, this could result in exclusion from services. However, staff members from Muslim FBOs reported that they are open to providing services to other groups, and they offered examples of how they try to avoid promoting Islam in their service provision in an effort to make others comfortable. "We have some Christian women who come here. These women, I think they feel comfortable here because we don't say anything about Islam, unless you say you want to be part of our special programs for Islam. And we don't ask you, you have to tell us you want to. So I don't think we have any problems from that. We also have some atheists here, some kind of people who don't believe in God, and I think they are comfortable too."

In addition, staff members both from the Muslim FBOs themselves and from other organizations indicated that the local Muslim FBOs have a high degree of collaboration with other NGOs, including FBOs of other faiths. In fact, most of the FBO staff who were interviewed indicated that their organizations cooperate with FBOs of other faiths; indeed, more than 80 percent of staff members reported collaboration with other FBOs. This high degree of cooperation would seem to suggest a genuine willingness to work with and serve other communities.

Given the fact that Bosnia and Herzegovina has a relatively inclusive and highly secular NGO sector, it seems that the risks of exclusion in service provision are comparatively low, particularly when compared to the case of Lebanon. In addition, although there are anecdotal reports of evangelism by FBO workers in Bosnia and Herzegovina, the interviews did not produce any evidence of this, and public discourse certainly lacks the anti-conversion fervor that exists in Sri Lanka. Therefore, it seems that the risk of coercion in service provision is low as well.

If anything, Bosnia and Herzegovina may have lessons to offer the NGO sector and particularly the FBO sector in other parts of the world. Naturally, it is important to note that Bosnia and Herzegovina's NGO sector is the product of a unique history of communism and war. NGO sectors in other countries would have neither the ability nor the desire to duplicate these specific conditions. However, the presence of and mentoring by international NGOs, and particularly international FBOs, seems to have had a positive influence both on public opinion and local NGO behavior. The Bosnian public has a positive impression of international Christian FBOs, and this positive impression may spill over into good will toward the Christian population in general. Perhaps more important, in spite of its initial reluctance, the local Catholic FBO in Bosnia and Herzegovina has become the most inclusive of the local FBOs from the country's three dominant faiths, thanks in no small part to pressure from its international Catholic FBO partners. Whereas Orthodox and Muslim FBO staff reported that more than 90 percent of their service recipients are from their own faith communities, the local Catholic FBO reports that its service recipients are between 60 and 70 percent Catholic.

Of course, the hopeful picture painted here does not mean that the NGO sector in Bosnia and Herzegovina is not at risk for exclusion in service provision. Inclusion has been protected by a highly secularized NGO sector and an active international NGO community, but these are not necessarily permanent features of Bosnian society. In particular, the international political, military, and humanitarian presence in Bosnian society is waning. Many international NGOs and FBOs have left Bosnia and Herzegovina or are planning to leave in the near future, as a consequence of both the growing stability in the country and the needs presented by disasters in other parts of the world. Meanwhile, local secular NGOs are highly dependent on an international donor community whose interests increasingly are being focused elsewhere in the world. Secular NGOs need to become more self-sustainable if the sector is to remain vibrant, and in the absence of foreign donors, unfortunately many secular NGOs and FBOs will cease to exist. One hopes that Bosnia and Herzegovina's NGO sector will continue to be large and strong, but in difficult times the local FBOs from the three dominant faiths may prove to be most resilient by virtue of their deep community roots and local institutional support. After all, these are the same FBOs that closed their doors for fifty years during communism, only to revive as soon as political conditions permitted.

Notes

1. For more on the complex relationship between faith and ethnicity in Bosnia and Herzegovina, see Stuart J. Kaufman, *Modern Hatreds: The Symbolic Politics of Ethnic War* (Ithaca, NY: Cornell University Press, 2001); Heather Rae, *State Identities and the Homogenisation of Peoples* (Cambridge: Cambridge University Press, 2002); and Stephen M. Saideman, *The Ties That Divide: Ethnic Politics, Foreign Policy, and International Conflict* (New York: Columbia University Press, 2001).

2. Demographic and geographic information is taken from the United States Central Intelligence Agency, *CIA World Factbook* (Washington, DC: United States Central Intelligence Agency, 2006).

3. Kaufman, 2001; Rae, 2002.

4. Kaufman, 2001; Rae, 2002; Saideman, 2001.

5. Kaufman, 2001; Rae, 2002; Saideman, 2001.

6. Rae, 2002. For more on rape as a tactic of war in Bosnia and Herzegovina, see Beverly Allen, *Rape Warfare: The Hidden Genocide in Bosnia-Herzegovina and Croatia* (Minneapolis: University of Minnesota Press, 1996); and Alexandra Stiglmayer, *Mass Rape: The War Against Women in Bosnia-Herzegovina* (Omaha: University of Nebraska Press, 1994). For more on refugees and persons internally displaced as a result of the conflict in Bosnia and Herzegovina, see United Nations High Commissioner for Refugees (UNHCR), *2005 Global Refugee Trends* (Geneva: UNHCR, 2005).

7. For more on the religious characteristics of the conflict in Bosnia and Herzegovina, see Michael A. Sells, *The Bridge Betrayed: Religion and Genocide in Bosnia* (Berkeley: University of California Press, 1998).

8. Allen, 1996; Rae, 2002; Saideman, 2001; Stiglmayer, 1994.

9. *Khomeinis* is a term referring to followers of Ayatollah Ruhollah Khomeini, the Iranian religious and political leader who in 1979 made Iran the world's first Islamic republic. *Mujahideen* is an Arabic and Persian word meaning "those who participate in struggle"; it is commonly used to refer to Muslim guerrilla fighters.

10. Rae, 2002; Saideman, 2001.

11. For more information on the composition of the NGO sector in Bosnia and Herzegovina, see International Council of Voluntary Agencies of Bosnia and Herzegovina (ICVA), *The ICVA Directory of Humanitarian and Development Agencies in Bosnia and Herzegovina* (Sarajevo: International Council of Voluntary Agencies, 2005).

12. For more on the influence of the communist period on the development of the NGO sector in Eastern Europe, see Adam Fagan, "Taking Stock of Civil-Society Development in Post-Communist Europe: Evidence from the Czech Republic," *Democratization* 12, no. 4 (2005): 528–47. For more on the unique philosophy during Tito's communist rule, see Thomas Oleszczuk, "The Liberalization of Dictatorship: The Titoist Lesson to the Third World," *The Journal of Politics* 43 (1981): 818–30.

13. International Council of Voluntary Agencies of Bosnia and Herzegovina (ICVA), 2005.

14. Tamsin Bradley, "Does Compassion Bring Results? A Critical Perspective on Faith and Development," *Culture and Religion* 6, no. 3 (2005): 337–51; Mark Chaves and William Tsitsos, "Congregations and Social Services: What They Do, How They Do It, and with Whom," *Nonprofit & Voluntary Sector Quarterly* 30, no. 4 (2001): 660–83; Helen Rose Ebaugh, Paula F. Pipes, Janet Saltzman Chafetz, and Martha Daniels, "Where's the Religion? Distinguishing Faith-Based from Secular Social Service Agencies," *Journal for the Scientific Study of Religion* 42, no. 3 (2003): 411–26; Robert Fischer, "In God We Trust, All Others Bring Data: Assessing the State of Outcomes Measurement for Faith-Based and Community-Based Programming," in *Innovations in Effective Compassion: Compendium of Research Papers*

Presented at the Faith-Based and Community Initiatives Conference on Research, Outcomes, and Evaluation (Washington, DC: US Department of Health and Human Services, 2008), 179–211; Byron R. Johnson, Ralph Brett Tompkins, and Derek Webb, *Objective Hope—Assessing the Effectiveness of Faith-Based Organizations: A Review of the Literature* (Philadelphia: University of Pennsylvania, Center for Research on Religion and Urban Civil Society, 2002).

15. Bradley, 2005; Chaves and Tsitsos, 2001; Ebaugh, Pipes, Saltzman Chafetz, and Daniels, 2003; Fischer, 2008.

16. Robert Wuthnow and Virginia A. Hodgkinson, *Faith and Philanthropy in America: Exploring the Role of Religion in America's Voluntary Sector* (San Francisco, CA: Jossey-Bass, 1990); Pui-Yan Lam, "As the Flocks Gather: How Religion Affects Voluntary Association Participation," *Journal for the Scientific Study of Religion* 41, no. 3 (2002): 405–22.

17. In July 1995, Serb forces overtook the United Nations "safe area" of Srebrenica and in five days killed a documented 7,475 Muslim men and boys. The massacre has been characterized as the worst in Europe since World War II. Some place the estimate of deaths at as high as 10,000 civilians, because almost 40 percent of Bosnians still missing and unaccounted for after the war are from the municipality of Srebrenica. For more, see Helge Brunborg, Torkild Hovde Lyngstad, and Henrik Urdal, "Accounting for Genocide: How Many Were Killed in Srebrenica?" *European Journal of Population* 19, no. 3 (2004): 229–48.

5

Faith-Based Organizations and Violence

The Broader Picture

The previous three chapters have presented country-specific examples of how religious identity influences the attitudes and behavior of FBO staff in contexts of violence—and how violence in turn has influenced the evolution and behavior of each country's NGO sector. But what characteristics do Lebanon, Sri Lanka, and Bosnia and Herzegovina share as a group, and what lessons can these cases provide for FBOs in the rest of the world? This chapter will present findings from the cases of these three countries in the aggregate, paying special attention to the sectarian nature of inclusion and exclusion in service provision, and will suggest implications for practitioners in the NGO community at large.

The Salience of Identity and Its Implications for Exclusion

This book is based in its entirety on interview data gathered from over one hundred staff members from seventy different NGOs. Sixty-three percent of these interview participants were from FBOs, and 37 percent were from secular NGOs. Seventy-two percent were from local, country-based NGOs, and 28 percent were from international NGOs with head-quarters in a country other than Bosnia and Herzegovina, Lebanon, or Sri Lanka. On the basis of answers to the interview questions, I coded whether interview participants indicated that either ethnic or religious identity influenced their attitudes toward service recipients and service provision. I also made note of whether interview participants indicated that they primarily served recipients of their same (or of a single) ethnic or religious group or reported serving an ethnically and/or religiously mixed group.

As Table 5.1 shows, the interview responses support the argument that when an NGO shares its identity with one of the groups involved in the local ethnic or religious conflict, staff members will indicate, during their interview, that the conflict-associated identity has a strong influence on their attitudes toward service provision. As was discussed in Chapter 1, this high identity salience among FBO staff members is to be expected because, just like everyone else in their communities, staff members are exposed to mechanisms that promote and channel collective violence. Of those participants whose NGO shared its identity with one of the groups involved in the conflict, 64 percent provided information demonstrating that the conflict-associated identity had a strong influence on their attitudes toward service provision. This figure would include, for example, an individual working for a Muslim FBO in Bosnia and Herzegovina who indicated that Islam had an important influence on his or her attitudes toward service provision. Thirty-six percent of those participants whose NGO shared its identity with one of the groups involved in the conflict did not provide such information. Among those participants whose NGO did *not* share its identity with one of the groups involved in the conflict, only 13 percent provided information demonstrating that the conflict-associated identity had a strong influence on their attitudes toward service provision, whereas 87 percent did not provide such information (see Table 5.1). It may seem illogical that individuals who did not share a conflict-associated identity were still influenced by the identity of the NGO, but the respondents in this category

Table 5.1 Influence of Conflict-Associated Identity on Staff Member Attitudes—Full Sample (n = 102)

Identity of NGO	Strong Influence		Weak/No Influence		Strong Influence of Another Identity	
	Number of participants	Percent of participants	Number of participants	Percent of participants	Number of participants	Percent of participants
Conflict-Associated	36	64%	20	36%		
Not Conflict-Associated	6[a]	13%	40	87%		
Other Excluded Group					7	100%

Note: a. This figure captures international NGO staff who may not be members of the groups involved in the conflict but are influenced by their own faith identity. For example, evangelical Christians in Lebanon, though not members of the local Christian denominations involved in Lebanon's civil war, are nonetheless highly influenced by their own Christian faith.

were mostly international FBO staff. For example, even though a Dutch staff member from an international Christian FBO would not share the same identity as Maronite Christians who were heavily involved in the Lebanese civil war, he or she might still be highly influenced by his or her Christian identity.

In addition, the interview data show that for some ethno-religious groups, the identity associated with the prominent local ethnic or religious conflict is not their most salient identity. Some groups have historical experiences of violence or exclusion that they consider to be more significant to their personal identity than, say, the Lebanese civil war, the conflict between the Sri Lankan state and the Tamil Tigers, or the Balkan conflict among Bosniaks, Croats, and Serbs. This makes sense because most people have multiple identities, and shared history of conquest or repression by culturally different peoples is one criterion that many ethnoreligious groups use to define themselves.[1] An example of this dynamic would be the case of Armenian Christian FBOs in Lebanon, which were discussed at length in Chapter 2. Although the conflict under consideration is the Lebanese civil war between Christian and Muslim militants, many people associated with Armenian Christian FBOs stated that their Christian identity had a less important influence on their work than their Armenian ethnic identity. Their historical experience of the Armenian genocide caused these groups to have a strong desire to promote and preserve Armenian language and culture as a part of their work, and these goals assumed at least as much importance as their faith-based goals. Under these circumstances, polarization and boundary activation still result in high identity salience. The interview data demonstrated that all individuals whose identity group had been targeted by other significant forms of violence and/or exclusion, such as Armenians and Palestinians, indicated that their identity influenced their attitudes regarding service provision (see Table 5.1).

The influence of identity on attitudes toward service provision is most visible if we remove secular NGOs and international FBOs from the sample and examine only local FBOs (see Table 5.2). It seems clear that one would expect staff from FBOs to be more influenced by religious identity

Table 5.2 Influence of Conflict-Associated Identity on Staff Member Attitudes—Local FBOs (n = 47)

Identity of NGO	Strong Influence		Weak/No Influence		Strong Influence of Another Identity	
	Number of participants	Percent of participants	Number of participants	Percent of participants	Number of participants	Percent of participants
Conflict-Associated	29	69%	13	31%		
Not Conflict-Associated	0	0%	5	100%		
Other Excluded Group					4	100%

than staff from secular organizations would be. One also would expect staff of local FBOs to be more influenced by the conflict-associated identity than staff of international FBOs. This is because interview participants from international FBOs, though they were not *always* foreign nationals, were more likely to be from a country other than the one where the research was conducted. Therefore, typically staff from international FBOs had not been affected personally by the polarization and boundary activation generated by the politics of collective violence. Second, as was discussed in previous chapters, participants from international FBOs were more likely to report that their organization had become secular over time, thus somewhat neutralizing the influence of religious identity on staff members.

When looking only at interview participants from local FBOs, of those participants whose FBO shared its identity with one of the groups involved in the conflict, 69 percent provided information demonstrating that the conflict-associated identity had a strong influence on their attitudes toward service provision. Thirty-one percent did not provide such information. All participants whose FBO did not share its identity with one of the groups involved in the conflict failed to provide information demonstrating that the conflict-associated identity had a strong influence on their attitudes toward service provision. Once again, all individuals whose identity group had been targeted by other significant forms of violence and/or exclusion indicated that their identity influenced their attitudes regarding service provision (see Table 5.2).

In line with the assertions made in Chapter 1, the data in the aggregate also support the argument that when an FBO shares the same identity as one of the groups involved in violent religious conflict, fewer community members with a different identity will seek services from, and/or be provided services by, that FBO. As we can see in Table 5.3, when an NGO shared its identity with one of the groups involved in the conflict under consideration, interview participants more often indicated that their organization provided services primarily to their own ethno-religious group. Of those participants whose NGO shared its identity with one of the groups involved in the conflict, 55 percent provided

Table 5.3 Influence of Conflict-Associated Identity on Service Provision—Full Sample (n = 102)

	Excludes Other Identity Groups		Includes Other Identity Groups	
	Number of participants	Percent of participants	Number of participants	Percent of participants
Conflict-Associated	31	55%	25	45%
Not Conflict-Associated	9[a]	20%	37	80%
Other Excluded Group	6	86%	1	14%

Note: a. Again, this figure captures international NGO staff who may not be members of the groups involved in the conflict but are influenced by their own faith identity.

information demonstrating that their organization provided services primarily to their own ethno-religious group. For example, this figure would include a staff member from a Buddhist FBO who indicated that his or her organization primarily served other Buddhists. Forty-five percent of those participants whose NGO shared its identity with one of the groups involved in the conflict indicated that their organization provided services to an ethnically or religiously mixed group. Of those participants whose NGO did not share its identity with one of the groups involved in the conflict, 20 percent indicated that their organization provided services primarily to their own (or a single) ethno-religious group, whereas 80 percent indicated that their organization provided services to an ethnically or religiously mixed group (see Table 5.3).

The interview data demonstrated that 86 percent of those whose identity group has been targeted by other significant forms of violence and/or exclusion indicated that their organization provided services primarily to their own ethno-religious group. This figure would include, for example, a staff member from a Palestinian NGO who indicated that his or her organization served only Palestinians. One individual whose identity group had been targeted by other significant forms of violence and/or exclusion indicated that their organization provided services to an ethnically or religiously mixed group (see Table 5.3).

Once again, the influence of identity on inclusion in service provision is more visible if we remove secular NGOs and international FBOs from the sample, and examine only local FBOs (see Table 5.4). In Table 5.4, one can see that identity is closely tied to exclusive service provision. Of those participants whose FBO shared its identity with one of the groups involved in the conflict, 71 percent provided information demonstrating that their organization provided services primarily to their own ethno-religious group, whereas 29 percent indicated that their organization provided services to an ethnically or religiously mixed group. Of those participants whose NGO did not share its identity with one of the groups involved in the conflict, all indicated that their organization provided services to an ethnically or religiously mixed group of recipients. All individuals whose identity group had been targeted by other significant forms of violence and/or exclusion indicated that their organization provided services primarily to their own ethnic or religious group (see Table 5.4).

It is important to note that the tables in this chapter are not intended to imply a robust statistical analysis. Clearly one would need a much larger sample from a broader array of countries to make such an argument. Rather, the tables are presented to make it clear that identity has important implications for exclusion from services in contexts of conflict. The interview data strongly support the assertion that the identity

Table 5.4 Influence of Conflict-Associated Identity on Service Provision—Local FBOs (n = 47)

	Excludes Other Identity Groups		Includes Other Identity Groups	
	Number of participants	Percent of participants	Number of participants	Percent of participants
Conflict-Associated	30	71%	12	29%
Not Conflict-Associated	0	0%	5	100%
Other Excluded Group	4	100%	0	0%

salience of FBO staff will be high in contexts of violence, and that FBO service provision in contexts of violence will be exclusive based on ethno-religious identity. This is particularly true when local FBOs are specifically examined. Even though interview data are by nature subjective and rely on the interview participants' truthfulness, it is reasonable to assume that participants who chose to be dishonest in their interviews would be more likely to overstate the inclusiveness of their organization, rather than claiming that their behavior was more exclusionary than it actually is. Therefore, if these data are inaccurate as a consequence of dishonesty, it probably would result in what statisticians call a Type II error. In other words, if the data are inaccurate due to dishonesty, reality probably provides even greater support than is apparent in the accompanying tables for the argument that identify salience leads to exclusion in service provision.

Whereas it may seem understandable that local FBOs would be exclusive in their service provision, what is perhaps more disturbing is the picture this information paints of international FBOs. The tables show quite clearly that the identity salience of local FBO staff is high in contexts of violence and that local FBO service provision in contexts of violence is exclusive based on ethno-religious identity, but strikingly, this pattern does not disappear when we look at the full sample. Although the pattern of exclusion is less pronounced, it is still present when we examine international FBOs. This is because the mechanisms that promote and channel collective violence not only influence the behavior of local FBO staff members, but also influence the behavior of the poor in communities that have experienced violent religious conflict. Thus, even though the staff of international FBOs may be relatively unaffected by local polarization and boundary activation, the mechanisms of collective violence are quite salient for the populations they seek to serve. Because boundary activation causes social interactions to organize increasingly around group identity, potential service recipients of other ethnicities and religions may be apprehensive about seeking services from an international FBO, even if the FBO would be willing to provide them with services. Potential service recipients assess whether international FBOs are socially located inside or outside activated boundaries, and then they decide whether or not to seek assistance from the organization. The result is that international FBOs are not immune to the politics of collective violence, even when they arrive from abroad with intentions of providing service equitably.

Implications for Practice

Prior pages may present a somewhat dismal portrait of religious exclusion in international development. However, because Soss's[2] research indicates that the experiences individuals have while receiving social services can have important repercussions for how they perceive and participate in government, there is reason to believe that inclusive service provision can have positive implications for recipients, even outside the service environment. Based on the specific findings from the three country cases, I have several suggestions for ways in which nonprofit managers and public and private donors/contractors can encourage more inclusive service provision by NGOs in the developing world. These include increasing the sustainability of local secular NGOs, encouraging relationships between local and international NGOs, increasing outreach and referrals among different ethnic and religious groups, initiating joint service provision by FBOs of multiple faiths, providing services in "neutral" locations with approval from "neutral" officials, and creating fair and balanced restrictions on proselytization.

Increase the Sustainability of Local Secular NGOs

Perhaps the most desirable, yet most challenging, way of increasing the inclusiveness of the NGO sector is to increase the sustainability of local secular NGOs. Decreasing dependency on foreign funding is critical. Many of the secular NGOs examined in this book were beginning to become involved in small-scale income-generating projects, which will no doubt be helpful in this regard. Increased technical assistance to NGOs involved in social enterprise can help improve sustainability. Increased contracting with local governments might also help, though such opportunities may be limited by the lack of state resources in many parts of the developing world. In addition, some interview participants expressed concerns about losing their autonomy when working too closely with government entities, and contracting relationships may not be desirable if NGOs have a contentious relationship with the state.

If NGOs are not able to become entirely independent of foreign funding, it is imperative that organizations that are currently focused on the needs created by local conflict begin to diversify their activities into other domains as violence abates. Donors become less interested in funding war relief and rehabilitation programs in some countries as new conflicts emerge, and many NGO staff mentioned suffering when funders shifted their attention to countries such as Iraq and Afghanistan. An interesting survival strategy evident in Bosnia and Herzegovina is that NGOs that have previously focused on women victims of war are now beginning to focus on other forms of violence against women, such as domestic violence and human trafficking. This shift in mission enables NGOs to continue to serve their populations while accessing new funding streams and new networks of expertise. Indeed, several interview participants told stories of NGOs that had ceased to exist because they were not able to redefine themselves as donor attention shifted away from local conflicts.

Encourage Relationships with International FBOs

The evidence from the Bosnia and Herzegovina case indicates that the international NGO community has benefited the local NGO sector by providing models of professional, inclusive service provision and assisting with local NGO capacity building. In particular, the inclusive mandate sent by the international Catholic FBO community to local Catholic FBOs has helped to enhance inclusion in the local FBO sector. Continued and increased cooperation with international NGOs—and particularly with international FBOs—may help to institutionalize a culture of inclusive service provision among local FBOs. These cooperative ties can be developed by both local and international nonprofit managers, and they can be encouraged with financial incentives in contracts and donors' grant agreements. Given that local church networks were one of the important faith-related benefits cited by international FBO staff, local NGOs undoubtedly will benefit international NGOs as well, with their grassroots connections and invaluable local knowledge.

The responsible departure of international NGOs from the country is critical to the success of the relationships between international and local NGOs. International NGOs may benefit the local NGO sector by providing models of professional service provision and assisting with local NGO capacity building, but they must continue and even increase this mentoring before leaving the country. Particularly in Bosnia and Herzegovina, staff members from international NGOs were well aware that they were likely to leave soon for Iraq, and these staff wanted to depart the country in a responsible manner, leaving behind sustainable programs. It is important that international NGOs continue to send a message of inclusive service provision, and thus help institutionalize this value within local NGOs, as they prepare to depart the country.

Increase Outreach and Referrals
Among Different Ethnic and Religious Groups

Most of the interview participants in all three countries, even from those NGOs that were exclusionary in their service provision, indicated that their NGO would welcome service recipients of other ethnic and religious groups. If this indeed is true, a strategy to decrease the risk of exclusion from services is to encourage NGOs to conduct outreach to members of other ethnic and religious groups and refer clients to NGOs from different groups, particularly if these NGOs are sole service providers. Such activities could help correct for the comparative disadvantage of some ethnic and religious groups as service providers, as well as reducing the potential coercive influence of sole service provision.

Nonprofit managers could undertake increasing outreach and referrals in a variety of low-cost ways. One simply would be informing

NGOs of other ethno-religious groups of the services they have available and encouraging referrals among the different NGOs. Because many NGOs of different faiths belong to local and national NGO councils that meet on a regular basis, these councils could serve as a venue for initiating such an outreach and referral process. Outreach also could be conducted through public awareness campaigns, though this might involve some cost to the organization. NGOs whose resources are already stretched thin may be leery of increasing their financial burden by including new service recipients from other sects, but these costs, as well as the costs of public awareness campaigns, could be offset by incentives from private sector and public sector donors and contractors.

Initiate Joint Service Provision by FBOs of Multiple Faiths

Another strategy to encourage inclusion in FBO service provision would be to encourage cooperative service provision by FBOs of multiple faiths. This may have a number of practical advantages, such as allowing FBOs to pool resources and share each others' expertise. And NGOs can maximize their impact and minimize the duplication of services and the tying up of valuable resources that might have been used in another manner.[3] But above and beyond these practical advantages, encouraging cooperation among multiple faiths may increase inclusion and decrease coercion in the provision of services in three specific ways. First, seeing providers of different faiths working together might make potential service recipients feel more confident that services are being provided regardless of religion, and they might therefore feel more comfortable seeking services from the FBOs.

Second, such measures may have the potential to increase intergroup understanding and reconciliation by improving public perceptions of the different groups involved and providing a valuable example of interfaith cooperation. A report by the United States Institute for Peace[4] notes the considerable weight that the actions of religious leaders carry in their particular communities; it even mentions the publicity that was generated in Bosnia and Herzegovina when two religious leaders from different groups were seen having coffee together in a public café. Bigger initiatives, on the order of providing social services together or coordinating short-term activities such as a one-day health fair, might do wonders by offering an example of intergroup reconciliation.

Third, providing services in the same physical location might create an environment of self-monitoring that could protect service recipients from coercion and evangelism, because staff from one faith may be less likely to proselytize under the watchful eye of their colleagues from another faith. Once again, these measures could be encouraged by donors and contractors. They could be encouraged with incentives from international donors, or they could be made a requirement for grant recipients.

Provide Services in "Neutral" Locations with Approval from "Neutral" Officials

Particularly in the case of Sri Lanka, the interviews indicated that services were often provided in houses of worship. In addition, service recipients' claims that they needed assistance often were subject to validation by local religious leaders. For example, if an individual claimed to have lost a fishing boat in the 2004 Asian tsunami, the FBO would ask a priest, monk, or imam to confirm that the individual indeed had owned a boat prior to the disaster. Both of these conditions seem to create an obvious risk of self-exclusion for those who are not members of the FBOs' religious group. Potential service recipients may be particularly fearful of exclusion from services or evangelism if they must seek services in a house of worship different from their own, and if their claims are subject to the approval of religious leaders from other groups. Moving service provision to a location that is not a church or other house of worship would ease the minds of individuals seeking assistance who may believe services are available only to members of that congregation, who are apprehensive about asking another religious group for assistance, or who are fearful of attempts at conversion.

Admittedly, for smaller FBOs that lack access to an alternative physical space, a change in the location of service provision may not be realistic.

However, for FBOs that have the physical space, providing services in a "neutral" location can greatly increase inclusiveness in service provision. Meanwhile, because religious congregations often have intimate knowledge of their own communities and of who is in need, it seems unreasonable to ask FBOs not to accept referrals from religious leaders. However, removing the power of giving the final stamp of approval from the hands of religious leaders would reduce the potential for exclusion and coercion when providing aid. Especially in contexts of past religious conflict, potential service recipients may be fearful that religious leaders from other groups will deny their claims in retribution for the past acts of their fellow adherents. Because most programs select their recipients in accordance with predetermined needs-based criteria, it seems reasonable to request that an FBO staff member who is not a member of the clergy make the final determination of the validity of individuals' needs for service.

Creating Fair and Balanced Restrictions on Proselytization

A final strategy that nonprofit managers can undertake to reduce self-exclusion and coercion in service provision is to create unambiguous organizational guidelines and prohibitions on proselytization, with clear consequences for violations of these guidelines. Obviously, FBOs that have an organizational goal of evangelism would not be interested in enacting such guidelines, so this suggestion is not aimed at those NGOs. However, past research on child welfare FBOs in Eastern Europe indicates that front-line NGO staff are often much more actively engaged in evangelism than nonprofit managers indicate is permitted within the organization.[5] For those FBOs that genuinely desire to provide services in a noncoercive manner, clear guidelines on proselytization and regular reminders of these guidelines to front-line staff are essential for promoting an inclusive service environment.

A desirable, but admittedly difficult, strategy for decreasing the risk of self-exclusion from services and the risk of coercion in service provision would be to enact legislation that prevents the exploitation of poor and vulnerable groups, while simultaneously protecting freedom of expression and freedom of religion. This has been attempted in Sri Lanka, but so far, the anti-conversion legislation proposed to the Sri Lankan Parliament has been politically charged and has contained clauses that undeniably violate basic freedoms. Most versions have required that people register any change in their religious affiliation with the government within a specified period of time or risk being fined. This unquestionably violates basic religious freedoms and rights to privacy. In addition, most legislation has included prohibitions on "allurement" that are so vague that almost any offer of assistance could be construed as an attempt to evangelize.

Given the great deal of positive work that FBOs do in Sri Lanka and worldwide, it undoubtedly would be a mistake to discourage their efforts to provide services. However, in a country where people are fearful of conversion, legal measures should be put in place to ensure that evangelism and aid are decoupled. Any legislation passed must ensure that the poor and those affected by war and natural disaster are not coerced and exploited, while simultaneously guaranteeing that individuals have the freedom to choose and change their religion as they wish. Without question, this is a delicate balance to strike.

Conclusion

From an intellectual standpoint, perhaps the most interesting aspect of this discussion is that, in a field often dominated by theories of altruism and positive forms of social capital, this book demonstrates the utility of enlisting concepts from the politics of collective violence as a lens for examining behavior in the nonprofit sector. The interviews offer evidence that the mechanisms that promote and channel collective violence also shape the behavior of nonprofit staff. Religious faith motivates philanthropy and generosity, but it also motivates violence and exclusion. As can be seen from the evidence yielded by these interviews, religious faith can promote sectarianism, and the organizations in this study often reinforced, rather than transcended, schisms found in the larger society where they work. Although the organizations in this study may have generated high levels of "bonding social capital within their own ethno-religious groups, there is little evidence of active attempts to generate "bridging social capital. Researchers of the nonprofit sector often can be the sector's most ardent cheerleaders. But as important as it is to acknowledge the positive impact that nonprofit organizations have on societies worldwide, it is to the detriment of both research and practice to ignore the darker aspects of NGO behavior.

It is important that practitioners, policymakers, and scholars give careful attention to NGOs operating in non-Western contexts and to the behavior of FBOs of non-Christian faiths. Theory regarding the nonprofit sector has undeniably been developed through a Western lens. Information on the nonprofit sector outside the United States is limited, and what little detailed information exists usually involves economically developed countries such as those in Western Europe and Japan.[6] The theories applied to the nonprofit sector often are based on assumptions of developed market economies, democratic political systems, and cultural traditions and social arrangements associated with Judeo-Christian religions. The use of these theories is questionable in societies where the market is poorly developed, where political and cultural traditions are different, and where a history of colonial rule has often distorted or destroyed indigenous forms of culture and sources of power.[7] This book provides evidence that the activities of nonprofit organizations have different implications outside the context of Western Europe and the United States and that they are influenced by the specific historical contexts in which the NGO sector evolved. We must continue to examine other important questions about NGOs, faith, and development, such as the dynamics of inclusion and exclusion in service provision in countries not affected by conflict, the impact of faith identity on the quality of services provided, and the perspectives of service recipients and potential service recipients on faith-based service providers.

In addition to having important implications for nonprofit managers and funders, I argue that recipients' experiences with service systems are important and should be of interest to policymakers. Concerns about distributive justice and the conviction that all human beings deserve to have their basic needs met regardless of ethnicity, faith, or other personal characteristics are paramount. However, it is also important to keep in mind that social welfare programs serve as sites for political learning[8] and that the nonprofit sector in general often serves as a vehicle for political participation.[9] In the context of international development, if potential service recipients are excluded by nonprofit service providers on the grounds of ethnic or religious identity, or if they feel that their ethno-religious identity is not respected as a consequence of being subjected to efforts at evangelizing, citizens' negative experiences as service recipients may cause them to view the state and the nonprofit sector as reinforcing and reproducing ethnic and religious divisions.

Equity guarantees are important in societies where political rights are often fledgling and poorly defined, and where religious, ethnic, or other sectarian divisions and conflicts exist. Some scholars suggest that citizens are at risk of losing basic political rights when universal services are delivered by NGOs, which are accountable to the state and their funders rather than directly accountable to the citizens who receive their services.[10] If NGOs step in to fill a void in services, they must also acknowledge their accountability to the people they are serving.[11] Although some would argue that nonprofit organizations intrinsically arise from the community and thus offer strong guarantees of responsiveness to citizens,[12] this book counters that in contexts of conflict, this responsiveness may be limited to those citizens with a shared religious identity.

Past research would lead one to believe that the experiences of citizens receiving development aid can have an important impact on their perception of, and engagement with, their own government and the civil society sector. Studies of social welfare systems in the United States indicate that recipients' feelings of efficacy and levels of political engagement vary across program designs. Service recipients who do not fear losing access to benefits perceive government as a whole as being more responsive and concerned with the needs of citizens. In addition, service recipients in systems that encourage client participation in decision-making processes have higher feelings of efficacy and higher levels of political engagement outside the service environment.[13] Therefore, policymakers and nonprofit managers are in a position to support and create programs that maximize both the political and the practical benefits of their services for recipients. If policymakers truly are concerned with creating effective democratic governments and vibrant civil societies in the developing world, and if foreign donor governments are interested in maintaining a positive image worldwide, they should have a strong interest in ensuring that individuals have fair and equitable experiences when they receive services. Reducing exclusionary or evangelistic practices by service providers can help to further the aim.

Notes

1. For more on the role that conquest or repression plays in the formation of minority group identity, see Ted Gurr, *People Versus States: Minorities at Risk in the New Century* (Washington, DC: United States Institute of Peace Press, 2000).

2. Joe Soss, *Unwanted Claims: The Politics of Participation in the U.S. Welfare System* (Ann Arbor: University of Michigan Press, 2002).

3. Carlo Benedetti, "Islamic and Christian Inspired Relief NGOs: Between Tactical Collaboration and Strategic Diffidence?" *Journal of International Development* 18 (2006): 849–59.

4. United States Institute of Peace (USIP), *Can Faith-Based NGOs Advance Interfaith Reconciliation? The Case of Bosnia and Herzegovina* (Washington, DC: United States Institute of Peace, 2003).

5. Shawn Teresa Flanigan, "Paying for God's Work: A Rights-Based Examination of Faith-Based NGOs in Romania," *VOLUNTAS: International Journal of Voluntary and Nonprofit Organizations* 18, no. 2 (2007): 156–75.

6. Lester Salamon, "Government-Nonprofit Relations in International Perspective," in *Nonprofits & Government: Collaboration and Conflict*, ed. Elizabeth T. Boris and Eugene Steuerle (Washington, DC: The Urban Institute, 1999): 31–67.

7. Helmut Anheier and Lester Salamon, *The Nonprofit Sector in the Developing World* (Manchester, England: Manchester University Press, 1998).

8. Soss, 2002.

9. Judith R. Saidel, "Nonprofit Organizations, Political Engagement, and Public Policy," in *Exploring Organizations and Advocacy*, ed. Elizabeth J. Reid and Maria D. Montilla (Washington, DC: The Urban Institute, 2002): 1–18.

10. Geof Wood, "States Without Citizens: Problems of the Franchise State," in *NGOs, States and Donors: Too Close for Comfort?* ed. David Hulme and Michael Edwards (London: Macmillan Press, 1997).

11. Peter van Tuijl, "NGOs and Human Rights: Sources of Justice and Democracy," *Journal of International Affairs* 52, no. 2 (1999): 493–512.

12. Ralph Kramer, *Voluntary Agencies in the Welfare State* (Berkeley: University of California Press, 1981).

13. Soss, 2002; Sidney Verba, Kay Lehman Schlozman, and Henry Brady, *Voice and Equality: Civic Voluntarism in American Politics* (Cambridge, MA: Harvard University Press, 1995).

Bibliography

Abul-Husn, Latif. *The Lebanese Conflict: Looking Inward*. Boulder, CO: Lynne Rienner Publishers, 1998.

al-Hout, Bayan Nuwayhed. *Sabra and Shatila: September 1982*. Ann Arbor, MI: Pluto Press, 2004.

Allen, Beverly. *Rape Warfare: The Hidden Genocide in Bosnia-Herzegovina and Croatia*. Minneapolis: University of Minnesota Press, 1996.

Ammerman, Nancy T. *Doing Good in American Communities: Congregations and Service Organizations Working Together*. Hartford, CT: Hartford Institute for Religious Research, 2001.

Anheier, Helmut, and Lester Salamon. *The Nonprofit Sector in the Developing World*. Manchester, England: Manchester University Press, 1998.

Bartkowski, John P. *The Promise and Peril of Charitable Choice: Faith-Based Initiatives in Mississippi*. Cambridge, MA: Harvard University Press, 2001.

Benedetti, Carlo. "Islamic and Christian Inspired Relief NGOs: Between Tactical Collaboration and Strategic Diffidence?" *Journal of International Development*, 18 (2006): 849–59.

Benthall, Jonathan, and Jerome Bellion-Jourdan. *The Charitable Crescent: Politics of Aid in the Muslim World*. New York: St. Martin's Press, 2003.

Bond, George D. *Buddhism at Work: Community Development, Social Empowerment and the Sarvodaya Movement.* West Hartford, CT: Kumarian Press, 2004.

Borstein, Erica. "Developing Faith: Theologies of Economic Development in Zimbabwe." *Journal of Religion in Africa* 32, no. 1 (2002): 4–31.

Bradley, Tamsin. "Does Compassion Bring Results? A Critical Perspective on Faith and Development." *Culture and Religion* 6, no. 3 (2005): 337–51.

Branch, Alvia Y. *Faith and Action: Implementation of the National Faith-Based Initiative for High-Risk Youth.* Philadelphia, PA: Public/Private Ventures, 2002.

Brunborg, Helge, Torkild Hovde Lyngstad, and Henrik Urdal. "Accounting for Genocide: How Many Were Killed in Srebrenica?" *European Journal of Population* 19, no. 3 (2004): 229–48.

Candland, Christopher. "Faith as Social Capital: Religion and Community Development in Southern Asia." *Policy Sciences* 33 (2000): 355–74.

Chandrakanthan, A. J. V. "Eelam Tamil Nationalism: An Inside View." In *Sri Lankan Tamil Nationalism: Its Origins and Development in the Nineteenth and Twentieth Centuries*, by A. Jeyaratnam Wilson, 157–75. Vancouver: University of British Columbia Press, 2000.

Chaves, Mark, and William Tsitsos. "Congregations and Social Services: What They Do, How They Do It, and with Whom." *Nonprofit & Voluntary Sector Quarterly* 30, no. 4 (2001): 660–83.

Chowdry, Kamla, and Wendy R. Tyndale. "The Sarvodaya Shramadana Movement." In *Visions of Development: Faith Based Initiatives*, edited by Wendy R. Tyndale, 9–16. Aldershot, England: Ashgate Publishing Limited, 2006.

Clark, John. *Democratizing Development: The Role of Voluntary Organizations.* West Hartford, CT: Kumarian Press, 1991.

Clarke, Gerard. "Agents of Transformation? Donors, Faith-Based Organsations and International Development." *Third World Quarterly* 28, no. 1 (2007): 77–96.

De Vita, Carol J., and Sarah Wilson. *Faith-Based Initiatives: Sacred Deeds and Secular Dollars*. Washington, DC: The Urban Institute, the Hauser Center for Nonprofit Organizations, 2001.

DeVotta, Neil. *Blowback: Linguistic Nationalism, Institutional Decay, and Ethnic Conflict in Sri Lanka*. Stanford, CA: Stanford University Press, 2004.

———. "Civil Society and Non-governmental Organizations in Sri Lanka: Peacemakers or Parasites?" *Civil Wars* 7, no. 2 (2005): 171–82.

Durkheim, Émile. *The Elementary Forms of the Religious Life*. New York: The Free Press, 1954.

Eban, Abba. *The Beirut Massacre: The Complete Kahan Commission Report*. New York: Karz-Cohl, 1983.

Ebaugh, Helen Rose, Paula F. Pipes, Janet Saltzman Chafetz, and Martha Daniels. "Where's the Religion? Distinguishing Faith-Based from Secular Social Service Agencies." *Journal for the Scientific Study of Religion* 42, no. 3, (2003): 411–26.

Emerson, Richard M. "Power-Dependence Relations." *American Sociological Review* 27, (1962): 31–41.

Fagan, Adam. "Taking Stock of Civil-Society Development in Post-Communist Europe: Evidence from the Czech Republic." *Democratization* 12, no. 4 (2005): 528–47.

Fischer, Robert. "In God We Trust, All Others Bring Data: Assessing the State of Outcomes Measurement for Faith-Based and Community-Based Programming." In *Innovations in Effective Compassion: Compendium of Research Papers Presented at the Faith-Based and Community Initiatives Conference on Research, Outcomes, and Evaluation,* 179–211. Washington, DC: US Department of Health and Human Services, 2008.

Fisk, Robert. *The Great War for Civilisation: The Conquest of the Middle East*. New York: Knopf, 2006.

Flanigan, Shawn Teresa. "Paying for God's Work: A Rights-Based Examination of Faith-Based NGOs in Romania." *VOLUNTAS:*

International Journal of Voluntary and Nonprofit Organizations 18, no. 2 (2007): 156–75.

Fox, Jonathan. "Religion and State Failure: An Examination of the Extent and Magnitude of Religious Conflict from 1950 to 1996." *International Political Science Review* 25, no. 1 (2004): 55–64.

Gurr, Ted. *People Versus States: Minorities at Risk in the New Century.* Washington, DC: United States Institute of Peace Press, 2000.

Harris, Margaret, Peter Halfpenny, and Colin Rochester. "A Social Policy Role for Faith-Based Organisations? Lessons from the UK Jewish Voluntary Sector." *Journal of Social Policy* 32, no. 1 (2003): 93–112.

Hasenfeld, Yeheskel. *Human Service Organizations.* Englewood Cliffs, NJ: Prentice-Hall, 1983.

Hasenfeld, Yeheskel. "Power in Social Work Practice." *Social Service Review* 61, no. 3 (1987): 469–83.

Hodson, Roland. "Elephant Loose in the Jungle: The World Bank and NGOs in Sri Lanka." In *NGOs, States and Donors: Too Close for Comfort?* edited by David Hulme and Michael Edwards. London: Macmillan Press, 1997.

Ilchman, Warren F., Stanley Katz, and Edward L. Queen II. *Philanthropy in the World's Traditions.* Bloomington: Indiana University Press, 1998.

International Council of Voluntary Agencies of Bosnia and Herzegovina (ICVA). *The ICVA Directory of Humanitarian and Development Agencies in Bosnia and Herzegovina.* Sarajevo: International Council of Voluntary Agencies, 2005.

James, Estelle. *The Nonprofit Sector in International Perspective: Studies in Comparative Culture and Policy.* New York: Oxford University Press, 1989.

Jeavons, Thomas. *When the Bottom Line Is Faithfulness: Management of Christian Service Organizations.* Bloomington: Indiana University Press, 1994.

———. "Identifying Characteristics of 'Religious' Organizations: An Exploratory Proposal." In *Sacred Companies: Organizational Aspects of Religion and Religious Aspects of Organizations*, edited by

N. J. Demerath III, Peter Dobkin Hall, Terry Schmitt, and Rhys H. Williams, 79–96. New York: Oxford University Press, 1998.

Johnson, Byron R., Ralph Brett Tompkins, and Derek Webb. *Objective Hope—Assessing the Effectiveness of Faith-Based Organizations: A Review of the Literature*. Philadelphia: University of Pennsylvania, Center for Research on Religion and Urban Civil Society, 2002.

Johnson, Michael. *All Honourable Men: The Social Origins of War in Lebanon*. London: I. B. Tauris, 2002.

Juergensmeyer, Mark. *Terror in the Mind of God: The Global Rise of Religious Violence*. Berkeley: University of California Press, 2003.

Kaufman, Stuart J. *Modern Hatreds: The Symbolic Politics of Ethnic War*. Ithaca, NY: Cornell University Press, 2001.

Kim, Kirsteen. *Concepts of Development in the Christian Traditions: A Religions and Development Background Paper, Working Paper No. 16*. Birmingham, England: Religions and Development Research Programme, University of Birmingham, 2007.

Kramer, Ralph. *Voluntary Agencies in the Welfare State*. Berkeley: University of California Press, 1981.

Lam, Pui-Yan. "As the Flocks Gather: How Religion Affects Voluntary Association Participation." *Journal for the Scientific Study of Religion* 41, no. 3 (2002): 405–22.

Macy, Joanna. *Dharma and Development: Religion as Resource in the Sarvodaya Self-Help Movement*. West Hartford, CT: Kumarian Press, 1985.

Manogaran, Chelvadurai. *Ethnic Conflict and Reconciliation in Sri Lanka*. Honolulu: University of Hawaii Press, 1987.

Marzouk, Mohsen. "The Associative Phenomenon in the Arab World: Engine of Democratization or Witness to the Crisis?" In *NGOs, States and Donors: Too Close for Comfort?* edited by David Hulme and Michael Edwards, 191–201. London: Macmillan Press, 1997.

McCleary, Rachel. *Internationalizing American Compassion: The United States Government and Private Voluntary Agencies in International Relief and Development, 1939 to Present*. Oxford, England: Oxford University Press, 2009.

McCleary, Rachel M., and Robert J. Barro. "Private Voluntary Organizations Engaged in International Assistance, 1939–2004." *Nonprofit and Voluntary Sector Quarterly* 37, no. 3 (2008): 512–36.

Monsma, Stephen V. *When Sacred and Secular Mix: Religious Nonprofit Organizations and Public Money.* Lanham, MD: Rowman and Littlefield, 1996.

Monsma, Stephen V., and Carolyn M. Mounts, *Working Faith: How Religious Organizations Provide Welfare-to-Work Services.* Philadelphia, PA: Center for Religion and Urban Civil Society, 2002.

Nichols, J. Bruce. *The Uneasy Alliance: Religion, Refugee Work, and U.S. Foreign Policy.* New York: Oxford University Press, 1988.

Obeid, Anis. *The Druze and Their Faith in Tawhid.* Syracuse, NY: Syracuse University Press, 2006.

Oleszczuk, Thomas. "The Liberalization of Dictatorship: The Titoist Lesson to the Third World." *The Journal of Politics* 43 (1981): 818–30.

Orjuela, Camilla. "Civil Society in Civil War: The Case of Sri Lanka." *Civil Wars* 7, no. 2 (2005): 120–37.

Parliament of Sri Lanka. *A Bill on Prohibition of Forcible Conversion of Religions.* Colombo: Parliament of Sri Lanka, 2004.

Picard, Elizabeth. *Lebanon: A Shattered Country.* New York: Holmes & Meier, 2002.

Rae, Heather. *State Identities and the Homogenisation of Peoples.* Cambridge: Cambridge University Press, 2002.

Renner, Michael. *Politicization of Aid in Sri Lanka Turns Deadly.* Washington, DC: Worldwatch Institute, 2006.

Reuter, Christopher. *My Life Is a Weapon: A Modern History of Suicide Bombing.* Princeton, NJ: Princeton University Press, 2002.

Rose-Ackerman, Susan. "Altruism, Nonprofits and Economic Theory." *Journal of Economic Literature* 34, no. 2 (1996): 701–26.

Sager, Rebecca, and Laura Susan Stephens. "Serving Up Sermons: Clients' Reaction to Religious Elements at Congregation-Run Feeding Establishments." *Nonprofit and Voluntary Sector Quarterly* 34, no. 3 (2005): 297–315.

Saidel, Judith R. "Nonprofit Organizations, Political Engagement, and Public Policy." In *Exploring Organizations and Advocacy*, edited by Elizabeth J. Reid and Maria D. Montilla, 1–18. Washington, DC: Urban Institute, 2002.

Saideman, Stephen M. *The Ties That Divide: Ethnic Politics, Foreign Policy, and International Conflict.* New York: Columbia University Press, 2001.

Salamon, Lester. *Partners in Public Service: Government-Nonprofit Relations in the Modern Welfare State.* Baltimore, MD: Johns Hopkins University Press, 1995.

———. "Government-Nonprofit Relations in International Perspective." In *Nonprofits & Government: Collaboration and Conflict*, edited by Elizabeth T. Boris and Eugene Steuerle, 31–67. Washington, DC: The Urban Institute, 1999.

Salamon, Lester, S. Wojciech Sokolowski, and Regina List. *Global Civil Society: An Overview.* Baltimore, MD: Johns Hopkins Center for Civil Society Studies, 2003.

Schneider, Jo Anne, Katie Day, and Gwynneth Anderson. *Connections Between Faith Communities and Their Non-profits. Findings from the Faith and Organizations Project Pilot Study.* Washington, DC: George Washington Institute for Public Policy, 2005.

Sells, Michael A. *The Bridge Betrayed: Religion and Genocide in Bosnia.* Berkeley: University of California Press, 1998.

Smith, Bradford, Sylvia Shue, Jennifer Lisa Vest, and Joseph Villarreal. *Philanthropy in Communities of Color.* Bloomington: Indiana University Press, 1999.

Smith, Steven Rathgeb, and Michael R. Sosin, "The Varieties of Faith-Related Agencies." *Public Administrative Review* 61, (2001): 651–69.

Soss, Joe. *Unwanted Claims: The Politics of Participation in the U.S. Welfare System.* Ann Arbor: University of Michigan Press, 2002.

Stiglmayer, Alexandra. *Mass Rape: The War Against Women in Bosnia-Herzegovina.* Omaha: University of Nebraska Press, 1994.

Thiagarajah, Jeevan, and Norbert Ropers. *An Annotation to the "Principles of Conduct for the International Federation of Red Cross and Red Crescent Societies/International Committee of the Red Cross and NGOs in Disaster Response Programmes."* Colombo: Consortium of Humanitarian Agencies and Berghof Foundation for Conflict Studies–Sri Lanka Office, 2005.

Tilly, Charles. *The Politics of Collective Violence.* New York: Cambridge University Press, 2003.

Treverton, Gregory F., Heather S. Gregg, Daniel Gibran, and Charles W. Yost. *Exploring Religious Conflict.* Santa Monica, CA: RAND Corporation, 2005.

Tyndale, Wendy R. *Visions of Development: Faith Based Initiatives.* Aldershot, England: Ashgate Publishing Limited, 2006.

United Nations High Commission for Refugees (UNHCR). *2005 Global Refugee Trends.* Geneva: UNHCR, 2005.

United States Central Intelligence Agency. *CIA World Factbook.* Washington, DC: United States Central Intelligence Agency, 2006.

United States Department of State. *International Religious Freedom Report 2005.* Washington, DC: United States Department of State, 2005.

United States Institute of Peace (USIP). *Can Faith-Based NGOs Advance Interfaith Reconciliation? The Case of Bosnia and Herzegovina.* Washington, DC: United States Institute of Peace, 2003.

van Tuijl, Peter. "NGOs and Human Rights: Sources of Justice and Democracy." *Journal of International Affairs* 52, no. 2 (1999): 493–512.

Verba, Sidney, Kay Lehman Schlozman, and Henry Brady. *Voice and Equality: Civic Voluntarism in American Politics.* Cambridge, MA: Harvard University Press, 1995.

Wanigaratne, Ranjith. "The State-NGO Relationship in Sri Lanka: Rights, Interests, and Accountability." In *NGOs, States and Donors: Too Close for Comfort?* edited by David Hulme and Michael Edwards. London: Macmillan Press, 1997.

Watkins, Laura. "Misreading Needs: The Question of Capacity Building and Local Participation Among Displaced Muslim Women in Puttalam District." *Civil Wars* 7, no. 2 (2005): 138–55.

Weber, Max. *The Sociology of Religion.* Boston: Beacon Press, 1963.

Weber, Stephen. *Perceptions of the United States and Support for Violence Against America.* College Park, MD: National Consortium for the Study of Terrorism and Responses to Terrorism, 2006.

White, Sarah, and Romy Tiongco. *Doing Theology and Development: Meeting the Challenge of Poverty.* Edinburgh: Saint Andrew Press, 1997.

Wilson, A. Jeyaratnam. *Sri Lankan Tamil Nationalism: Its Origins and Development in the Nineteenth and Twentieth Centuries.* Vancouver: University of British Columbia Press, 2000.

Wood, Geof. "States Without Citizens: Problems of the Franchise State." In *NGOs, States and Donors: Too Close for Comfort?* edited by David Hulme and Michael Edwards. London: Macmillan Press, 1997.

Wuthnow, Robert. "Altruism and Sociological Theory." *Social Service Review* 67, no. 3 (1993): 344–58.

Wuthnow, Robert, and Virginia A. Hodgkinson. *Faith and Philanthropy in America: Exploring the Role of Religion in America's Voluntary Sector.* San Francisco, CA: Jossey-Bass, 1990.

Index

About the Author

Shawn Teresa Flanigan is an assistant professor of public administration in the School of Public Affairs at San Diego State University.
Her research focuses on the role that nonprofit organizations play in
meeting the health and social service needs of minorities and marginalized groups, with a specific interest in the developing world and low-
income populations in the United States.

Also from Kumarian Press...

Culture and Development:

Twinning Faith and Development:
Catholic Parish Partnering in the US and Haiti
Tara Hefferan

Buddhism at Work: Community Development,
Social Empowerment, and the Sarvodaya Movement
George Bond

Development and Culture
Edited by Deborah Eade

Development Brokers and Translators:
The Ethnography of Aid and Agencies
Edited by David Lewis and David Mosse

New and Forthcoming:

Snakes in Paradise: NGOs and the Aid Industry in Africa
Hans Holmén

Civil Society Under Strain:
Counter-Terrorism Policy, Civil Society and Aid Post 9/11
Edited by Jude Howell and Jeremy Lind

Building Peace: Practical Reflections from the Field
Edited by Craig Zelizer and Robert Rubinstein

Rights-Based Approaches to Development:
Exploring the Potential and Pitfalls
Edited by Diana Mitlin and Sam Hickey

Visit Kumarian Press at **www.kpbooks.com** or call **toll-free**
800.232.0223 for a complete catalog.

WITHDRAWN

 Kumarian Press, located in Sterling, Virginia, is a forward-looking, scholarly press that promotes active international engagement and an awareness of global connectedness.